EMPIRE'S ORPHAN

FROM HABSBURG AUSTRIA TO NEW YORK

BERNARD F. HERBERICK

D. HERBERICK

Published by Hospitality of Abraham, LLC

CONTENTS

PREFACE

Albertina Zimmerman (1856–1940) traversed the Atlantic from Habsburg Austria to New York during the latter days of the Empire. Imperial balls, *the* premiere of *Die Fledermaus,* and impromptu visits from Bohemian composer Bedřich Smetana—and more—were recounted to her grandson, Bernard F. Herberick. Whether hyperbole or fact, the romance of those days captured the lad's imagination and imbued in him an appreciation for culture—music, theater, dance, and cuisine.

Indeed, Mr. Herberick started his elementary education in America around 1915. However, his substantive, early, and informal education with his grandmother—his Oma—spanned from early childhood to adulthood, well beyond his university training at Fordham and Georgetown.

Much of his original manuscript of the memoir "Oma," written during the Cold War, is retained here and supplemented with historical and geo-political detail worth revisiting.

GROWING UP

SILESIA - TROPPAU - VIENNA

The molten lead froze in curious, fantastic shapes as it was poured out upon the hearth. In the flickering firelight, the gypsies[1] knelt shoulder to shoulder to study each sinuous curve and contour of the cooling metal. Seemingly satisfied with their inspection, they withdrew to a far corner to hold an animated whispered conference. Finally, when all the kerchiefed heads nodded in agreement, the eldest came forward to tell what the coming year was to hold for each of us.

— OMA

I remember listening to Oma as she relayed the magical stories of the gypsies. Like a photograph in sepia becoming animated, my imagination curved in shapes of fantastical images as her words transported me—I could touch the molten forms with my eyes and feel the silence of the bystanders waiting for the outcome of the gypsy elders' whispers. And Oma was living in that world again every time she sat me down and shared these moments with me. I could hear the rustle of her dress when she was still a beautiful young woman watching the gypsies. And I could sense a longing in her voice for life elsewhere that she had to depart, despite her smile and merry coal-black eyes.

My beloved maternal grandmother, "Oma," otherwise known as Albertina Zimmerman, lived during the grand old Austrian days of the Habsburg Empire. Her life and times captivated my imagination for the mere 30 years we shared.

Oma told me of the molten lead pouring tradition with its predictions, held regularly on New Year's Eve. She used to witness the gypsies performing the rituals of lead pouring at their grand Austrian manor house as a child. The wonder and amazement Oma experienced as the family contemplated the truth in the gypsies' predictions for the coming year came vividly alive for me. How exciting it must have been! Half doubting, half believing, to wonder if what the gypsies said would really come to pass.

She was describing *Bleigiessen*, better known as "lead pouring," a New Year's tradition where friends and family gather to practice predicting the coming year's fortune—or misfortune!

Bleigiessen is also known as *Molybdomancy* and is still practiced today in northern European countries, the UK, Austria, and Germany. A small piece of lead is melted over a candle and then poured from a spoon into the cool water. The hardened shape, which the lead takes on almost immediately, indicates what the year has in store for you. These shapes are interpreted in various ways, depending on your geographical location. Meanings associated with the figures are probably derived from what the gypsies ascribed in Oma's day: An elephant shape means someone will walk over you; an eagle, that you are ambitious; and so on.[2]

* * *

OMA'S YOUTH played out against the backdrop of the Habsburg monarchy, which aimed to govern most of Europe at the time.

The Silesian region that Oma knew was situated between Poland, Germany, and Bohemia (now better known as a part of Czechia and former Czechoslovakia) on the upper parts of the Oder river. Silesia is now mainly divided into four Polish provinces. The German, Czech, and Polish influences remain. During the 14th century, Silesia became a part of the Roman Empire before it passed to the Habsburgs in 1526. Some duchies remained under Polish rule until the 1700s.

The complex political insecurities and history tossed the region between Germany, Hungary, and Prussia for many years during the 1500s, with the Habsburg monarchy always having a firm hold on the region. During the 18th century, it was the richest of the Habsburg's Austrian provinces, with flourishing industries in mining and textiles. Because of this prosperity, the Prussian state annexed the region after the Silesian wars in 1742, and Silesia eventually became part of the German Empire in 1871.

Many languages infiltrated the population, with Polish and German remaining the two major academic languages until this day. The result is a diverse population with diversified social and cultural elements, cuisine, costumes, and architecture. Between and after World War I and II, Silesians were again tossed between various countries, mainly Czechoslovakia, Poland, and Austria. The Allies made Silesia part of Poland—again—and after the 1945 Potsdam Agreement, it was under the communist regime of the USSR.

* * *

OMA, KNOWN THEN AS "TINA," was born to a distinguished family in Silesia. She was christened Albertina—honoring Queen Victoria's prince consort, Albert of Saxe-Coburg.[3]. She was orphaned at an early age. First, her father passed away, then, shortly after, her mother. Oma's aunt was instructed by her mother to send the girl to a French convent school near Troppau, where she was forced to wear a grim uniform and adhere to strict discipline. Oma's mother was highly impressed and charmed by stories of the French soldiers of Napoleon who marched *en route* to Russia. She thought they were "gallant" and decided that her daughter had to be schooled in the same culture and language. Oma always used to say throughout her life that German "strikes the ear too harshly," preferring French above her native language.

* * *

NAPOLEON'S TOP SOLDIERS, the *Grande Armée*, were an elite corps of men who had to meet strict requirements. This unit also operated as a separate unit under a senior official and included troops from various European countries. This unit marched through Austria *en route* to Russia, which impressed Oma's mother greatly. However, history made a devious turn in Russia. Napoleon's army (who mistakenly thought the Russian invasion would only last for 30 days) was exposed to the merciless Russian army at the time. The French army suffered a loss of 400,000 men and thus signaled the beginning of the end of Napoleon's military reign.

* * *

AT TROPPAU, Oma discovered her taste for finery. This was becoming a controversial topic at the time because of its idle luxuriousness, but plumed and feathered hats caught her attention. Oma loved them so much that she decided to become a *"modiste"* where she could "swim in a sea of beautiful hats," and when she turned sixteen, she left her classes forever behind her and used a portion of her first inheritance to turn her dream into a reality.

* * *

THE GEORGIANS (1714–1837) and Victorians (1837–1901) followed Marie-Antoinette's iconic fashion trends regarding plumed hats. Some of these hats were so elaborate that they even flaunted whole birds atop the wearer's head. The demand for feathers ran many bird species to the brink of extinction. A flamboyantly plumed hat became the envy of many women in fashion centers like Paris and Vienna and across the globe in America, where they also became the height of fashion.

Peacocks, garden fowl, and pheasants were hunted and killed randomly for their beautiful feathers. Some of the most sought-after feathers were from ostriches, and at the time, these birds were still wild and had to be hunted to obtain their plumage. By the mid-19th century, ostriches were close to extinction in North Africa. More exotic species from South America, Southern Asia, and Guinea (like parrots and egrets) faced the same fate, as their worth was much higher than silver.

By the 1850s, feathered hats were not only worn by the wealthy aristocracy, but they were gradually becoming more commonplace. At this time, some people started lobbying against the cruelty of the fashion trend and its unsavory demand. It is said that the leading ornithologist, Frank Chapman, spotted more than three-quarters of the ladies' heads adorned with elaborately plumed hats in 1886 while taking only two walks in New York's upmarket shopping districts (Smith, 2021, para. 16).

The counterargument was that birds naturally molted their feathers, that birds existed in abundance, or that the human sense of fashion reigned supreme over nature. But, a few years before the turn of the century, campaigns and lobbying groups started to protect the birds, and in 1921, international legislation was finally established to ban feather imports. This plumage trend faded with the austerity owing to World War I and the inconvenience of donning an adorned hat inside modern, hooded automobiles.

* * *

OMA SET off gaily to Vienna and indulged in a marvelously unbridled shopping spree. Soon after, the boxes, trunks, and bags filled with finery arrived to make her dream come true in Troppau (present-day Opava in the Czech Republic). Fittingly, the German meaning of Troppau is "too much." Oma filled her luggage with enough hats to open her own shop there.

A modiste was a fashionable dressmaker during the 19th century. Impressionist artists like Edouard Manet produced exquisite paintings of devoted French *fashionistas* of *haute couture* with plumed hats and elaborate dresses. The fashion of the Habsburg era in Austria-Hungary at the time had its unique style, not far removed from the French. The upper-class Hungarian and Austrian ladies were well-informed about the fashion trends in France, and they upheld an accent of well-tailored elegance.

During the 18th century age of enlightenment, a global wave of leading political and economic world players envisioned and initiated change. Colonial expansion encouraged new continental links and brought the east and west closer to each other. This influenced fashion styles, especially with the aristocracy, who set the pace and example. Habsburg fashion can be described as exotic glamor. The Viennese succumbed to the enticement of foreign products, imported materials, and foodstuffs: "Far Eastern porcelain together with lacquer furniture and silk wall-hangings were the epitome of luxury" (The World of the Habsburgs, 2022). This enchantment spilled over to their dress sense.

To understand the fashion sense of Oma's 19th-century world, remember that the Austro-Hungarian elite portrayed their women as vulnerable and delicate in the chivalric world of their men. The Habsburgs (and Viennese) women dressed in feminine pastel-colored fabrics trimmed with lace, ribbons, and delicate flowers to enhance their fragility. "They seemed as delicate as pale flower petals and appeared in sharp contrast to the strong vibrancy of their uniformed protectors" (Metropolitan Museum of Art & Blum, 1979). There was a strong sense of romance to their fashion, and it's no wonder that Oma was delighted by both fashion worlds that she engaged in—the French extravagance of modern style laced with the splendor, charm, and elegant Austrian sense of chivalric fantasy and romance.

* * *

IT WAS ALWAYS SO easy to entice Oma's gaiety of memory. I merely had to play (or name) an operetta to tap into her elegant and joyful memories of bygone days. While Oma unfolded her exotic stories, I imagined sharing moments with her watching a Russian ballet and the Imperial Ballet of Saint Petersburg ballerinas or sharing her box at the Volksoper and State Opera.

Vienna, where operas, operettas, musicals, and ballet were performed at The Volksoper after it opened its doors in 1898. It became an exclusive music theater between 1903–1950, and during the years around World War I, it was known as the second-most prestigious opera house in Vienna. After World War II, it became the alternative venue for the ruined State Opera.

The State Opera was a magnificent, splendidly decorative, light, spacious entertainment venue. Today, it is still a place infused with comfort. Opera performances had already started during the reign of Emperor Leopold I (1757–1705), who was fond of music. Even though he had the typical "Habsburg lip," he played the flute and the spinet well. Lansdale noted in 1902:

The present Opera House's exterior, which began in 1861, is not especially impressive. Five unimposing statues, wearing an air of excessive ennui, are stationed between the square columns of an Italian loggia and constitute the chief decoration of the facade. The two architects, van der Nüll and Sicardsburg, both came to untimely ends before the completion of the building—one shot himself from chagrin at the sinking foundation, and the other died of mortification caused by the severe and quite unjust criticisms of the Viennese press. The interior, however, fully atones for any disappointment one may feel at the exterior. Regarded from a practical standpoint, it is unsurpassed. Three thousand spectators can be accommodated comfortably, each well-seated and commanding an uninterrupted view of the stage—one of the largest in Europe (para 10).

Until this day, the props and costumes are still provided by the "Imperial Arsenal" and its magnificent collection. Ballet at the opera house produces ballerinas of unique gracefulness and true beauty trained to perfection. Their costumes are exquisitely designed and dazzlingly worn during performances of the highest standard.

Vienna State Opera House (*Mayer/Unsplash*).

The Habsburg dynasty narrative stretched over more than 600 years (1278–1918), producing a string of royalty who reigned over vast areas of Europe, including Spain, Portugal, Hungary, Croatia, Bohemia, Austria, Austria-Hungary, lower provinces of Italy, and even abroad in Mexico. Their territorial gains were expansive, but they remained close through frequently arranged marriages. They expanded their powerful influences through political gains and established positions in the upper hierarchy of the church.

Because of the frequent inbreeding, the Habsburg's gene pool produced distinct facial deformities of the nose, jawline, and lower lip, which became known as the Habsburg nose, jaw, or lip. It is said that their gene pool also deteriorated to such an extent that it affected their demise. Their deposition from Austria and Hungary as rulers happened after their defeat in World War I, and they were banished from Austrian territory.

The Habsburgs, like Oma, were polyglots. Some of them spoke not only German but also French, Latin, Italian, and Czech. They were mainly fluent in these languages and were taught to speak them from infancy. Some even spoke Basque, Spanish, and Dutch. It is said that Charles V wittily remarked, "I speak Spanish/Latin [depending on the source] to God, Italian to women, French to men, and German to my horse" (Wikipedia Contributors, 2019). Franz Joseph also spoke Hungarian and Polish and expanded his linguistic proficiency by learning Latin and Greek.

* * *

OMA BROUGHT her stories to me, and they came alive as I sat by her feet by the hour, holding her hand, charmed and spellbound by all the grandeur and exotic tales laced with joy and love. To me, she was a grande dame of the Habsburg Empire. My favorite memory of her was a bright and animated old lady, plagued by arthritis but holding an old heirloom heart filled with music. She looked out upon life with her face etched by years of smiling, her undimmed mind, and her exquisite sense of humor—unscathed by sorrow while she told me of the Viennese life she knew so long, long ago.

Albertina Zimmerman, beloved Oma (Courtesy of the McCourt Collection).

HERRSCHAFTHAUS

BRUCKSTEINE

Oma did open her shop, but fate had another plan: Anton Zimmerman.

I fondly recall Oma's stories about their meeting and her youthful times. The shopgirls called her to take a look at "the most eligible bachelor in the region." "Too old!" thought Oma. She remembers thinking, how would anyone want anything to do with someone as old as he! But Oma's aunt acted swiftly as an intermediary, and the wedding and dowry were arranged after the first encounter.

Habsburg culture inspired and influenced married life at the new manor house for Oma. Historically, nobility marriages were mainly arranged to secure geographical, political, and ecclesiastical connections. Although these were primarily happening in royal households, they also influenced the rest of society. They confirmed and regulated foreign policy and maintained international stability. The Habsburg monarchy's various dynastic lines of arranged marriages secured many thrones for them after 1800 in Europe. According to Heinz Duchhardt, "the impression of a *great family of European dynasties* still prevails" even today to maintain their exclusivity (Duchhardt, 2011).

Marital unions were rarely influenced by happiness or affection, but social prestige and capital were significant factors in determining marital connection. These marriage agreements established the financial security of the brides, and so, for both parties, it meant a future investment of some sort, despite the lack of affection in many of these cases.

Grandfather Anton Zimmerman (Courtesy of the McCourt Collection).

The dowry concept that Oma was subject to has an almost 3,000-year history dating back to Babylonian times. It's a monetary amount or asset the bride brings to the marriage table as a gift to her husband. The intention for it was threefold: It gave some security to the bride should anything go wrong with the marriage, a considerable dowry served as an enticement to the potential groom, and it also established a "start-up" for setting up a home together.

Anton was nearly four times her age, but with the "arrival of spring, the month of the bride waltzed in." Oma said, "His youth went back so far in time that, as a young boy, Grandfather had worn powder in his hair." Customs in that part of Silesia took forever to change, and velvet, candlelight, and Rococo traditions lingered long in the *Ancien Régime*.

I formed my impression of Grandfather Anton from a photograph of him standing behind Oma with a possessive hand on her shoulder. My perception of him was two-dimensional: a resolute, formidable old gentleman with a frock coat and sponge-bag trousers. Unlike Oma, he took a dim view of the dances and energy of Strauss II. In Anton's opinion, "If a deaf man were to observe waltzers, he would think he was seeing monkeys jumping about, not supposedly civilized human beings."

Viennese composer and waltz king Johann Strauss II (1825–1899) needs no introduction. His most famous works are *The Blue Danube* (a rolling waltz still played on famous town squares in Europe) and *Die Fledermaus* (*The Bat:* a classical Viennese operetta). He was the eldest son of composer Johann Strauss I, who didn't want his three musically talented (and only legitimate) sons to become musicians! However, Strauss Junior studied the violin secretly and became one of the most noteworthy composers after his father's death. His brilliant music career spans more than 40 years, while he directed his orchestras with his violin in one hand and the bow in the other. The ballroom dancing that his music inspired submerges anything else up to date.

He was charismatic and inspired many other well-known composers, and he quickly entered the global music scene with his unique compositions.

I cannot imagine Oma agreeing to Grandfather's view of one of her most joyful pleasures. Her personality connected closely with the fashion and creative melody of the Strauss II compositions. I also recall the gaiety of Oma's stories about Grandfather's slow plodding (one step at a time) as he ascended the stairs of the big manor house at Brucksteine while telling her that she "will also age" and she responding gaily to him "never!" —only to realize much later in life that he was actually correct.

* * *

GRANDFATHER'S ancestral manor home was Schloss Brucksteine. Bruckstein today is, as it was then, a small village now known as Mrokocin, situated in southwestern Poland. Mrokocin lies close to the current border of Hungary, with access to either Prague or Vienna. The 2011 census count tallied 160 inhabitants with a gradually decreasing population density of ~5% from 2000 to 2015. During Oma's time, there were even fewer inhabitants.

The Manor House at Brucksteine (*Maras/Polska.org.pl.*).

The *Herrschaftshaus* was an imposing country manor house with 40 bedrooms among its amenities. The building was situated elegantly on a prominent rise and overlooked the village and *gesinde* houses of the tenants and artisans. It had a sweeping vista of the broad acres of the fertile European landscape.

The rural house servants of a landlord in the 19th century were called the *gesinde*. In noble homes, they were called *hofgesinde*. Remuneration was mainly in the form of a small wage, a servant house or accommodation on the premises, and natural compensation in the form of food produced on the premises. Many of the *gesinde* were quite young, and some servants as young as 12 were working. A generally verbal collective agreement established the contract, which handed over monetary payment. Servants were often paid with products of their own work and, in many cases, inferior products. The landlord had the privileged freedom of choice to dismiss a servant at random.

Oma transformed her *Herrschaftshaus,* the former bastion of the bachelor, into an inviting home for society and gaiety. She added her feminine touch to the interior and livened up the rooms. It became a place where music and laughter filled the rooms while it housed a constant stream of visitors—relatives, friends, priests, students, and so forth—who came to stay for long periods. Transportation was complicated then, and the guests' slow and uncomfortable journey necessitated more extended visits. These were sometimes up to a month in length.

One occasional and unpredictable caller was the Bohemian composer Bedřich Smetana. Deafness and approaching madness made his visits memorable. "Usually, I had no inkling of his coming until I was awakened at two or three in the morning by an uproar in the music room. Grandfather would turn to me and say, ' Smetana has come.' Then we would try to sleep as best we could."

While the composer of the Bartered Bride would arrive unheralded, his departures were sometimes equally abrupt, disappearing without warning. "Later, I would learn that he had been upset by his bed not being turned down to his satisfaction or a favorite picture had been replaced. At other times, he was a gracious and considerate guest."

Bedřich Smetana (Allstar Picture Library Ltd/Alamy).

Bedřich Smetana (1824–1884) was a Bohemian composer of operas and famous symphonic poems like The Moldau. Often considered the father of Czech music, he was also the founder of the Czech national school of music and the first important nationalist composer of Bohemia. Smetana was a virtuoso piano player who performed for the first time in public at the mere age of six. He opened a piano school in 1848 in Prague, encouraged by his mentor, Franz Liszt, and was the conductor of the Swedish Gothenburg philharmonic society from 1856–1861. He also led the opening of the national opera house in Prague. His compositions established him as a distinctive Czech composer. Sadly, as Oma noted, he suffered from intense depressive states and showed symptoms of mental instability— and he eventually entered the Prague asylum, where he died.

Prodaná nevěsta (The Bartered Bride) is a three-act comic opera with which Smetana aspired to establish the operatic genre in true Czech spirit. It was his second opera (written in 1866) and not immediately favored by the public but only in later years. After a few adaptations, it became a global success. The literal translation is "Sold bride," but in the English tongue, the name "Bartered bride" was eventually taken. The story is set in a rural village and relays the frivolities of how true love prevails despite the preventative efforts of parents and the scheming of a marriage broker. It was also the first Czech opera performed more than a hundred times during the composer's lifetime. Smetana's Bohemian musical language expressed joy and happiness in dancing and festivity.

Oma had a deep affection and respect for the Habsburgs. Thinking they were enlightened rulers, she couldn't understand why Smetana wanted Bohemia's independence. She contended the Bohemians needed the Habsburg guidance; otherwise, they would only create problems for themselves that they would need help to resolve. One such issue was Czech nationalism.

She fitted all Europeans into her pigeonholes of opinion: Russians were "moody and utterly unpredictable," and the Prussians were "given to shouting and invariably humorless." The Poles were "happily confused," and the Hungarians "temperamental." The French, however, were a "cultural and thoroughly charming race," in Oma's opinion. But, the monarchist Oma wasn't much disturbed by Smetana's views. His firm nationalist belief found creative ground in his musical compositions, of which The Moldau is probably the most famous.

The Moldau (in Czech: Vltava) is one symphony poem of the musical series My Country (Má vlast) by Smetana that evokes the flow of the Vltava river with its source in the Bohemian mountains. A symphony poem is a tone poem (or musical composition) of a single movement for an orchestra with an inspirational story at its core. It is played in a natural sequence to a series of events. This patriotic work that captures Smetana's deep love for his homeland premiered in Prague on November 5, 1882. Smetana composed his series of six poetic movements—while slowly turning deaf—based on the landscapes and legends of his homeland, and he called them "musical pieces of Czech glories and defeats" (Schwarm, 2019). Each movement is a symphonic poem in itself with its own unique story. The Moldau is the second movement portraying rural scenes of the meadowlands' beauty and became the most popular part of the composition.

* * *

OMA'S TOLERANCE for Smetana's radical views was rooted in her passionate love for music. She had a childlike rapture similar to the pulsating violins of the gypsies, who also delighted her. Therefore, the gypsy nomads were always welcome at Brucksteine. The Brucksteine life was feudal, with locally manufactured produce and household paraphernalia from the estate itself. Many things were locally made, produced, and copied from Viennese and Parisian magazines, while all the food and wine, apart from special delicacies, came from Grandfather's estate.

However, shopping was a different story and almost an affair of state. Standing in line was unthinkable, and servants were sent to inform the shopkeepers of Oma's arrival. Then the store would be closed for other customers, so Oma could peruse and purchase at leisure. Jewelers and goldsmiths were summoned to the house when prospective purchases of items were needed to match her magnificent wardrobe.

* * *

HOUSE SERVANTS' qualifications were extraordinary and were mainly accepted on appearance instead of abilities. Oma believed that someone with a pretty face could be educated and trained to her liking, so attractiveness was the cue for an appointment at Schloss Brucksteine. "If they were pretty, they could be taught what to do. There is nothing more disconcerting than to see an unattractive face upon awakening," said she. So, qualifications came second. Male servants wore purple livery with black frogs and facings only when important guests were expected. The uniform was removed immediately after the guests' departure. The male servants were selected purely based on the sizes of livery available.

At the time, Black servants were unique, and Oma learned of her neighbor Baroness von der Recke's appointment of a Black coachman. This was an object of great curiosity because Black people were unknown in Central Europe then. Oma, of course, felt she simply had to meet the situation! After word was dispatched to Vienna, Oma's carriage did not only have a Black coachman, but she also sported a Black footman. She nodded courteously to her rival neighbor as their carriages passed one another.

* * *

THE AWARENESS OF A "BLACK" person in pre-21st century Europe has been interrogated over the past few decades, though the history remains somewhat hidden. Some facts stand out: What may appear a racist issue to our 21st-century perception was often not the case in the years preceding the 20th century. People at the time were more concerned about class differences than skin color differences. So, the documented traces of when and how Black people started to appear in Europe may remain vague, apart from instances associated with the slave trade. Furthermore, it seems that Black people were more prominently based in southern Europe, like Portugal and Spain, with only limited traces of a few hundred Black people in northern countries like Germany and Russia.

Olivette Otele, the author of African Europeans: An Untold History, argues in her article about the history of Black people in Europe that looking through the "prism" of colonialism and the slave trade only prevents people from realizing that African people have been present in Europe long before that (UNESCO Courier, 2021). She elaborates by saying that African ancestry can be traced back to the Roman empire: Emperor Septimius Severus (145–211) was the first African-born Roman emperor, and St. Augustine (354–430) who left a vast theological legacy was born in North Africa. The introduction of African people continued with their employment in court and with wealthy families in Sicily and Italy.

It has been noted that African people arrived in Europe regularly from the middle of the 15th century, mainly via the cross-cultural Mediterranean inter-ethnic space. The Lisbon court of Austrian Queen Catherine (1507–1578) lists the use of different ethnic domestic servants who were mainly women and children. Black slaves were considered prestigious, provided social distinction, and could be seen as part of the imperialistic progress of a country. Although the appearance of Black people in Italy presents a complicated picture, it still calls attention to their introduction mainly through the slave trade. Slave trade from the East was prominent during the late 1400s but replaced by the trade of African slaves after the fall of Constantinople in 1453. Evidence of African presence in Europe is found in many Dutch and Italian Renaissance art, of which the Adoration of the Magi (1520) is probably the most well-known.

Tawreak Gamble-Eddington qualifies the existence of Black "otherness" in his honors thesis, The Black Experience in Mid-20th Century Great Britain, France, and Germany: The Positioning of a Community as the "Other," wherein he argues some discrimination and social stigmatization during the earlier Black presence in Europe (Gamble-Eddington, 2021):

> The Black experience in Europe is often not one that can be seen as merely black and white. Instead, it is a complex story of struggle, persecution, the yearning for acceptance, and a constant requirement to satisfy the needs of White mainstream society in Europe.

On the other hand, Professor Allison Blakeley of Boston University postulates that many of the Black people employed by the wealthy in early modern Europe lived well compared to the lower classes. Many times, their children were able to join the upper classes and even the aristocracy. So, it becomes evident that African (and Black) people were introduced to Europe over a more extended period than expected. Most importantly, some were not merely domestically employed but had significant societal roles, albeit as outsiders during later centuries.

Given the limited numbers of Black people in northern Europe at the time, Oma's appointment of the Black coachman and footman was a prestige play in a battle of appearances against her perceived rival, the Baroness von der Recke.

TO THE MANOR BORN

BRUCKSTEINE

*T*o this prosperous yet self-contained and peaceful world of Oma's new life, three children were born: Two sons, Johann (Hans) and August, and a daughter Crescentia —my mother. They were all tutored by a French governess and registered at birth at institutions of higher education. Hans in Göttingen[1] and August in Würzburg.[2] Admittance to these "better" schools in those days was through bloodlines, not academic tests or qualifications.

August, Crescentia, and Hans (Courtesy of the McCourt Collection).

My mother was sent to a "Higher Daughters" finishing school, which was the fashionable and prestigious thing to do then.

The *Höhere Mädchenschule* or *Töchterschule* were schools of higher education for girls in German-speaking countries. The first of these schools was founded at the beginning of the 1700s. It was mainly intended for girls of the wealthy bourgeoisie and aimed to prepare them to become wives and mothers by teaching them appropriate social graces. Wealthy families sent their girls to "finishing" schools (*Mädchenpensionat*) where they could also engage in academic subjects of a more scientific nature. However, the academic education of girls was not encouraged at the time, and secondary and tertiary education only became instrumental much later. The primary goal was to promote and prepare girls to find a husband.

Albertina and Hans (Courtesy of the McCourt Collection).

Hans, the eldest, evidently led a roistering life as a university student. He promptly joined a drinking and dueling society and soon acquired the necessary saber cuts, then the marks of a gentleman. She saw to it that Hans always had a valet (who, she suspected, occasionally took his place in the larger classes) and a handsome mastiff. One of the servant's duties was to carry packages, however small, for Hans—and to remain a respectful distance behind. This, Oma thought, was only as it should be. She did, however, object strenuously to the dog: "Such an expense to feed!

While Hans loved conviviality, younger brother August was introspective and studious and later became a curator of a university library

During World War I, Hans served as an officer with a cavalry regiment on the Eastern front. He was twice severely wounded and twice won the Iron Cross. Perversely, Oma took particular pride in one of his relatively trivial "exploits." As his unit prepared to pass through a Russian village, Hans noticed that its single street was filled with garbage and all manner of house-hold discards. He ordered the villagers out to sweep the streets clean. He permitted his horses to pass through with hooves unsoiled only when this business had been done to his satisfac-tion. It is axiomatic that calvary men, like movie cowboys, regard their mounts with great affection and are much concerned for their well-being. Oma viewed the incident as one stemming entirely from her training, seeing that "everything was clean and orderly."

In later years, I was amused no end by some of the everyday eccentricities of my two bachelor uncles. Hans was particularly stuffy with his pince-nez, close-cropped hair, walking stick, and heel-clicking. On greeting my sister, he never addressed her by name. He kissed the hand of the "The Miss Daughter."

I was "The Mr. Son" and given a correct stiff bow (instead of a handshake).

During one of his visits to our home in the United States, Hans placed his shoes outside his bedroom door. Since our house was not blessed with shoeshine facilities, the shoes remained unpolished. In the morning, he complained bitterly to my mother about the lack of service. She reacted rather strongly. Afterward, the shoes remained inside the bedroom.

August was cast in much the same mold. Mother had a pair of red shoes. When she appeared wearing them, August refused absolutely to act as her escort. "No one wears red shoes on the street in Vienna!" Mother capitulated. August was slightly less stiff in that he addressed me as "Herr Bernard." Two carry-overs from another world and another age!

Hans Zimmerman (Courtesy of the McCourt Collection).

I remember Mother tried to send money to her brothers in East Germany after World War II. It was confiscated by the US government. It took a long time to release the funds, and they were not supposed to do that right after World War II.

EVER-RELIABLE, UNFAILING CURE

VIENNA

*O*ma's training and interest in music continually drew her from Brucksteine to Vienna. She recalled with mischievous relish how she sometimes managed such visits. "The smell of paint caused me to have severe headaches. Just before some important musical event, painters appeared, as if by magic." A trip to Vienna was the ever-reliable and unfailing cure.

The Vienna of the 1880s she knew as a young woman was a splendid imperial city and the most sophisticated capital in Europe. It was the wellspring of some of the world's greatest music. Memories of Mendelssohn, von Weber, and Chopin were still fresh. Brahms, Liszt, Franck, Wagner, and others who were to become music's immortals were frequently seen strolling along the Ring, in their carriages in the Prater, in the the audience, or on the podium of the opera and concert halls.[12] The younger Johann Strauss reigned as the undisputed "Waltz King."

Position, taste, and means enabled her to move in elegant Viennese circles. Friendship, particularly with Strauss and Smetana, brought her into the world of composers and performers. Entree to court bails at the Hofburg and Schönnbrunn was provided by documented lineage. A brother-in-law, a colonel in one of the Guards regiments, was conveniently available. His son, a junior Guards officer and thereby automatically one of the "Weiner Edelknaben," was her frequent escort.

On the other hand, she found contact with businessmen invariably depressing. "They talked only of making money and did so with an almost unbelievable intensity."

Invitations to the Imperial balls were issued primarily based on family background. At least sixteen generations with the word "von" as part of the family name were required to make it to these invitations. Other invitations were only issued when an individual had served the Empire with unusual distinction or to visiting dignitaries.

As Oma shared her stories with me, it brought me close to her circle and life in 1880s Vienna while my imagination time traveled with her. In my imagination, our ages did not differ, and I could transform myself into the dashing Guards officer on her arm with my white Hussar's uniform, complete with the fur-trimmed tunic and gold lacings. Oma's delicate hand would hover demurely on my arm, and we would set off to a court ball at the Schönbrunn, Hofburg, or Belvedere.[345]

When Oma shared the glamor of these places with me, I imagined her plum-colored silk gown setting off her admirable wasp waist and her whispering with gaiety in her eyes: "It took two maids to lace me up" behind her fan. I imagine myself beside her, and instead of wearing her dust cap, her head would be crowned with her glorious dark blonde ringlet hair, with a nodding plume feather as the final accent to her ensemble. She would be moving gracefully (with the pains of arthritis still only a remote impossibility) while her heirloom heart would beat gaily again. I could sense my writing on the thin ivory pages of her dance card while congratulating myself on having such an exquisite partner. Oma was, as a young woman, indeed bewitchingly beautiful.

* * *

A DISTANT COUSIN was one of the ladies-in-waiting to the beautiful Empress Elisabeth. Ladies-in-waiting are women of noble birth who accompany a female monarch and assist her with intimate and personal tasks like bathing and dressing. They spend most of their day with their queen or other persons of royalty and, to that end, maintain a prominent role in public. Many royals have more than one lady-in-waiting and sometimes up to one hundred to assist them.

The Empress and Emperor (Sueddeutsche Zeitung Photo/Alamy).

EMPRESS ELISABETH (1837–1898) is considered one of the most beautiful queens ever. She was unusually tall for the time at 1.72 m (almost 5 feet and 8 inches) and had a slender and elegant appearance. She did not follow traditional fashion slavishly. Her magnificent mane of chestnut-colored hair framed her flawless complexion. She believed in understated natural beauty and maintained her appearance with subtle enhancement and care, which presented her with an aura of beauty that was rare and unpretentious at the time. Later in life, she preferred not to be painted and appeared publicly behind a veil.

She was the Consort of Emperor Franz Joseph and known formally as the Empress of Austria and Queen of Hungary, but lovingly known as Sisi to her family. Most notable was her care-free childhood and unconventional upbringing that was unusual for people of her royal status at the time. She lived with her parents in Munich, and at Possenhofen, their summer residence on Lake Starnberg, and the easy-going nature of her youth and close connection with her siblings remained her source of strength throughout her life.

Elisabeth, the daughter of Duke Maximillian and Princess Maria Ludovika from Bavaria, married Franz Joseph, a distant cousin, at the Augustinerkirche, Vienna, in 1854. Married life was challenging for Elisabeth. She said, "Marriage is an absurd institution. One is sold as a fifteen-year-old child and makes a vow one does not understand and then rues for thirty years or more and cannot undo" (Mutschlechner, 2023a, para.1).

The Viennese court was a highly institutional convention that operated under strict rules. Elisabeth, on the other hand, was an intelligent and sensitive young woman who did not value the etiquette and court formalities expected of her. She displayed empathy for the people and their suffering, and this sensitivity slowly alienated her from courtly life in Vienna.

Before 21, she had borne three children but was deprived of being involved with their upbringing. She became very depressed, further exacerbated by the death of her nearly two-year-old daughter, Sophie, in 1857. Sadly, Franz Joseph was emotionally divided between his loyalty to her and his mother, who imposed most courtly requirements. These events prompted her transformation into an independent woman, years of restless traveling to "recover her health" abroad, and disregarding convention. It is said that her husband often encouraged her return—and that he may have loved her more than she loved him.

Nevertheless, she lived a mainly alienated and isolated life as the wife and mother of Habsburg royalty, hence her transformation into a young independent—and at times quite eccentric —woman of her time. After the tragic suicide of her son, Rudolf, she became increasingly melancholic, always appearing in black, as she increasingly withdrew from public life. Her only political ambitions were focused on her affinity with Hungary, which she enthusiastically loved. Her youngest daughter was raised in Hungarian culture and language.

Empress Elisabeth, known as Sisi to her family (Library of Congress).

Elisabeth's life represents the changing 20th-century Habsburg decline. She gained cult status during these revolutionary times, enhanced by her tragic assassination in Geneva by the Italian anarchist Luigi Lucheni in 1898. Hadley Meares sums up the sad story of her life in *History* (Meares, 2018):

The unusual entrance into public life was one in a string of tragedies that marked Sisi's reign, placing her within a long line of reluctant royal consorts trapped in gilded cages. Isolated in the palace, she suffered through mental illness, mourned her beloved son's suicide and set off to wander the globe in search of peace—all before her assassination at the hand of an Italian anarchist (para. 1).

* * *

ONE OF OMA'S most significant encounters happened during a ball at the Hofburg. The Empress made her entrance through an avenue of bowing guests. As she reached Oma, Elisabeth paused, raised Oma's bowed head, and murmured, "Charming, my dear," before she passed on. After this, Oma became passionately devoted to the Empress and her life from that moment on. Every tragedy that struck the Empress's life became a tragedy to Oma's own heart. She was prostrate with grief when Elisabeth's brother-in-law Maximilian was executed in Mexico in 1867 and the Crown Prince, Rudolf, died a romantic suicide in 1889 at the imperial hunting lodge at Mayerling.

Ferdinand Maximilian Joseph (1832–1867) was Austria's Archduke and Mexico's Emperor. His naive liberal views and external political and imperialistic scheming ultimately brought him to the executioner's hand in brutal struggles in Mexico. He was the younger brother of Franz Joseph and served in the Austrian navy as rear-admiral and governor-general of the Lombardo-Venetian region.

The tragic death of Crown Prince Rudolf (the only son and heir to the throne of Franz Joseph and Elisabeth) has been much disputed and documented. Many years after his passing, it was only established that his death was a murder-suicide pact with his young mistress, the 17-year-old Baroness Marie von Vetsera. Despite all the controversy surrounding the death of the heir to the throne, his parents—and particularly Elisabeth—were devastated by the death of their liberal-thinking 30-year-old son. This event was said to have influenced the political upheaval between Austria and Hungary, eventually leading to World War I.

When Elisabeth herself was assassinated in 1898 while disembarking from a lake steamer in Geneva and heading to her next ship, Oma was deeply affected.

Empress Elisabeth's tragic life ended while she was visiting Geneva incognito. Her assassin had come to act against the ruling class, intending to show his protest by assassinating Prince Henri of Orléans. At the time, anarchy against the ruling class had ended the lives of a Russian czar, an Italian king, Spanish premiers, and a French president. So, when Lucheni discovered his intended victim canceled his journey, Elisabeth became the next best target. She was en route to board her ship when the incident took place. She initially thought it was merely a blow to her chest, and she proceeded to the vessel, where she succumbed to internal bleeding from the triangular file stabbing wound.

* * *

OMA MENTIONED the name of Franz Joseph with hushed reverence. Franz Joseph (1830–1916) was born (and died) in the Schönbrunn palace, leaving the Habsburg reign a mere two years in the hands of his grand-nephew before its collapse at the end of World War I in 1918. The Emperor outlived several big tragedies (the early death of his first child, the execution of his brother, his son's suicide, and the assassination of his beloved wife Sisi) before also enduring the assassination of his nephew Archduke Franz Ferdinand. He even survived an assassination attempt on his own life during his reign. His monarchy was troubled by nationalism throughout, and the Sarajevo assassination of his nephew activated a series of events that led to World War I. However, despite all the political difficulties he faced (and often took personally), he remained highly respected and held the Austrian Empire together while politicians squandered and squabbled it away. "Franz Joseph seemed to embody the empire so much that it inevitably had to perish with him," says Björn Rosen in the Tagesspiegel (Rosen, 2016).

He is lovingly remembered as the last monarch of the Habsburg dynasty (maintaining the longest Habsburg reign in history). He left an undeniable legacy in Vienna by giving his stamp of approval to many developments of the late 1800s. From a young age, he saw his mission as the patriarchal head of the family as a divine opportunity, and he served with humility while maintaining a noble distance. However, it is said that his inflexible traditionalism was instrumental in the collapse of the monarchy. His militaristic upbringing had a marked influence on him throughout his life, and wearing a uniform became his preferred attire. This habit, in fact, saved his life with the attempted assassination. He was known for being frugal and stoic but generous toward the ones he loved. His modesty and integrity were characteristics that followed him, and he was perceived in the public eye as a kind of relic, "a tower of strength." Because of his tragic life, the famed image of him became prominent as the Emperor being "spared nothing."

Franz Joseph's successor, the Archduke of Austria-Este and designated heir to the throne, Franz Ferdinand, represented feudal Austria with a narrow-minded conservative perspective. Born in Graz in 1863, he became the preferred heir after the tragic suicide of Crown Prince Rudolph. His father was Franz Joseph's brother, Karl Ludwig, who died in 1896, after which the young Archduke became the official heir to the Habsburg throne. Archduke Karl was a devout Catholic: Franz Ferdinand received a strict clerical upbringing combined with the typical military training that came with the Habsburg dynasty.

Archduke Franz Ferdinand (Chronicle/Alamy).

Nephew and Uncle had a tense relationship characterized by many arguments and an antagonizing lack of understanding between them. This was rooted in their opposing characters: Franz Joseph was mature, modest, and self-controlled, while Franz Ferdinand appeared impulsive and unpleasant. The more liberal Franz Joseph deliberately excluded the young and conservative Franz Ferdinand during critical political decision-making processes. Franz Ferdinand lacked diplomacy and aimed to uphold the former imperialistic dynastic clan with its aristocratic lifestyle and was thus not a popular figure in Viennese society with his anti-democratic viewpoints. "He vehemently opposed modernist tendencies, the industrial age, and middle-class parliamentarianism" (Mutschlechner, 2023g).

His opposition to the early Viennese modernist movement was also pronounced in his approval of architectural designs and personal art displays. He was an enthusiastic collector of art and held a vast collection of art and antiques even though he only sometimes carried the expertise to make wise purchasing choices which resulted in the procuring of many forgeries. He was the owner of the prized and most important Este art collection. He restored his residence at Upper Belvedere Palace to its former classic Austrian Habsburg style with many neo-Baroque features and *objets d'art*.

He loved hunting and was known as the trigger-happy Habsburg. The thrill of the hunting chase exposed his pathological character patterns as he kept meticulous hunting ledgers of his record-breaking 274,511 kills and displayed his hunting trophies in dense exhibits on his palace walls.

The differences between Franz Joseph and Franz Ferdinand became known as the intergenerational House of Habsburg conflict, and it played out between their residential palaces. Franz Joseph and his traditional court elites were at Schönbrunn, while the Belvedere became the symbol of a place where Franz Ferdinand could hone in his group of supporters against the "old gentleman at Schönbrunn."

Franz Ferdinand was a firm opponent of the Hungarian compromise, and he promoted his pro-Slav political plans of inclusion and deeper involvement. In addition, he also favored the German-Austrian and Magyar (Hungarian) ethnic groups, but he vehemently opposed the federalization of the Monarchy. His foreign policies often incorporated cooperation with Germany and reconciliation with Russia intending to create a long-lasting alliance between the conservative monarchies of Europe. He was ironically portrayed as the Balkan warmonger in the press even though he advocated a more moderate and less expansive foreign policy. He also opposed any intentions of aggression aimed at Italy and Serbia. However, his interest in the Balkan developments eventually led to his assassination, which triggered the world into a full-scale war. After this event, the world changed forever, something that Franz Joseph tried hard to prevent.

Archduke Ferdinand's assassination was one of the immediate causes of World War I. He was the son of Franz Joseph's younger brother Karl. Both Franz Ferdinand and his wife, Sophie, succumbed at the hands of the 19-year-old Bosnian Serb activist Gavrilo Princip when the latter assassinated them in Sarajevo on June 28, 1914. This event triggered a range of global events that ultimately led to Austria-Hungary's allies' war declaration against Serbia's allies—leading to World War I.

Franz Joseph himself died before his beloved Austro-Hungarian Empire disintegrated. His 68-year reign shaped the image of imperial rule and established Vienna as a pivotal metropolis in a multinational state extending from Hungary through Italy into the southern parts of Europe. His death sparked another period of intense mourning for Oma.

* * *

THE RUSSIAN CZAR once paid a visit to the Austrian Emperor. Vienna donned her most elegant finery for his visit: Fireworks, parades, and a general *éclat* honored the important guest. The highlight of the visit was a gala at the State Opera. To offer an unusual experience, the streets leading from Hofburg to the Opera were covered with salt. Thus, the Czar could drive the Emperor in his magnificent sleigh. Oma, and all of Vienna, was much impressed by this lavish show of wealth. However, only later was she appalled at the enormous waste of salt when she learned how precious and sorely needed this life-sustaining commodity was among the Russian peasantry.

After the galas in Vienna, a series of similar (but saltless) events were staged in Budapest. The Emperor hosted them this time in his role as King of Hungary and wearer of the Iron Crown of St. Stephen (or Holy Crown of Hungary), and Oma was "naturally required" to proceed to Budapest. She had also been on intimate terms with the Esterházy women who were guests during the gala.

* * *

ELITE AUSTRIAN SOCIETY subscribed to a strict hierarchy. A small group of noble families, fewer than 400, comprised the first tier. This socially exclusive group's most important family names were Liechtenstein, Schwarzenberg, Lobkowicz, and the Esterházy family. They established an aristocratic oligarchy with influential positions and privileges at court. This network of a tightly closed society managed to secure their marital, political, and financial security for many centuries, maintaining exclusivity and showcasing their noble elegance through their wealth. They erected a barrier between themselves and the rest of society. Their aristocratic roots—carefully examined by the head chamberlain—were the precondition for an invitation and connection to court. This first-tier social system lasted until the end of the monarchy in 1918.

Only the highest-ranking aristocracy was invited to evening balls during winter and spring, while the ladies met at salons, where they could appear without an official invitation, to reinforce their strong bonds of hereditary nobility. The Esterházy family was one of the most prominent in these circles.

The Esterházy family is one of the oldest in Hungary, dating back to the 13th century. Their Hungarian roots (from the northern parts of the country, when they married into wealthy families) continue despite numerous upheavals, deportations, and imprisonments after World War II. Many diplomats, counts, princes, nobility, military officers, and patrons of the arts come from the Esterházy families, who always remained loyal to the Habsburgs.

The wealthy Esterházys enjoyed feudal splendor by owning more than a hundred villages and one million acres of land where they built their 30 lavish residences, according to David Pryce-Jones's review of Victor Sebestyen's book about Budapest (Pryce-Jones, 2022, p. 39): "When a well-known British agriculturist told one of the Esterházys that he had 11,000 sheep, the prince replied that he had the same number of shepherds" (para. 6). During the 18th century, they were known as the largest landowner magnates in Hungary, and their private fortune appeared to be even more significant than the Habsburgs. They were so well positioned in society that they even had a cake named after them: The Esterházy Torte was named after Miklós and his brother Pál Antal. The former was so wealthy that he built a palace known as the Hungarian Versailles.

Princess Theresa Esterházy, one of the two most famous dynastic princesses, was said to be the most beautiful lady of Europe in the 19th century. Oma often commented that Hungarian women (particularly the Esterházy women) were among the most beautiful in the world. Still, she considered the Esterházy men "excellent judges of good horses and bad women!"

B18rucksteine was also situated in an area noted for its horses. The estate stables had animals for farm work and riding and matched pairs for carriages. Oma was also an excellent horse-woman who took particular delight in the performances and Lippizaner stallions of the Spanish Riding School in Vienna. She equated their graceful performance to the best of opera, ballet, or symphony. The horse riding was within the Hofburg complex, complete with the imperial box, magnificent crystal chandeliers, and carefully tended tanbark.

* * *

THE WORLD KNOWS Austria as the land of *Apfelstrudel, Sacher torte, Krapfen, Knödel* of all sorts, and *Kipfel* (which found its way to Marie-Antoinette's rooms in Versailles as the *Croissant* or *Brioche*). Visiting some of the finest culinary institutions in Vienna takes one back to the time when slow eating and culinary delights were savored as one of the most important events of the day. Der Demel and Hotel Sacher still rank top of the list after all these years, and the pleasure of whipped cream master-pieces can still be found there.

Der Demel had some tumultuous events since its inception in 1786 but maintained its high standard of being the royal purveyor and the only one to deliver to the Hofburg theater. The Demel family upheld its prestige over the years, even after the fall of the Austro-Hungarian Empire, and they remained owners of the business for almost two centuries. Der Demel lures tourists from all over the world with its playful displays and delicacies.

Perhaps Oma tasted the Esterházy cake or Sacher Torte there when she frequented the historical café—one of the rendezvous sites for high society. Oma recalled that "anyone demanding service was immediately and thoroughly ignored" because "people of quality always have time!" The delicacies of Der Demel and Hotel Sacher topped *bit schlag* on their delicious culinary creations and wreaked havoc on the wasp waists, which were the height of fashion at the time.

* * *

THROUGH OMA, I first became aware that there were two composers named Strauss. The father and son were bitter rivals primarily because Strauss senior did not encourage the musical career of his son Strauss junior. He insisted that his son become something more "sensible," like a lawyer. I also learned from Oma that Buda and Pest were initially separate cities.

Oma's memories of Johann Strauss II gave me a warm feeling when she talked about him. I understood that he was a friend of a friend. When I once listened to one of his waltzes with her, she commented: "You know, Sharni wrote that." I tried to argue with her by saying it was written by the famous younger Strauss, and all she said was, "Yes, Sharni. We all called him Sharni." He arranged her *loge* at the premiere of *Die Fleder-maus*. She recalled that the operetta wasn't well received at the time. Empress Elisabeth was seriously ill with typhoid, and Vienna was concerned for her welfare. Elisabeth recovered, and Die *Fledermaus* became the bright and tuneful classic it remains today.

Johann Strauss II (history_docu_photo/Alamy).

Oma explained that the royalty of the "waltz succession" probably began in earnest with Lanner, who wrote hundreds of polkas and waltzes, including the popular *Die Schönbrunner*.

* * *

JOSEPH FRANZ KARL LANNER (1801–1843) was an Austrian self-taught violinist and composer (and Sharni's predecessor). Strauss senior (one of the musicians in his orchestra) and Lanner shared the musical stage many times. Still, their artistic opinions eventually aggravated their friendship, causing their separation and the birth of their rivalry. However, Strauss I and Lanner left a significant mark on developing the new music genre with their compositions. Strauss I composed the *Radetzky March*, which at the time was probably the most well-known waltz in the world, but Lanner's *The Schönbrunner* was considered the most beautiful waltz for many years. He is mainly remembered as one of the earliest composers who turned the waltz's peasant form into a version enjoyed and accepted by the high Viennese society. His musical legacy left a string of polkas and waltzes for the world to enjoy.

Johann Strauss eventually took over his title of waltz king. The elder Strauss wished his son to be spared the anguish of a musician's life and was furious when Johann II announced his interest in a composition and conducting career. As mentioned earlier, he insisted that he become something sensible, like a lawyer, and that his younger son, Josef, become an engineer. But both boys studied music secretly, and with their mother's approval, Johann II began composing and forming his own orchestra while Josef followed his father's wishes. Josef invented the mechanical street sweeper before succumbing to the lure of the waltz. Sharni later said that his brother Josef was the more talented son of Johan Strauss I.

Oma was connected to this musical culture. She recalled Sharni's observations on his visit later to the US. Upon arriving in Boston, Strauss was greeted by a nerve-shattering rendition of his *Blue Danube,* and cannons fired in three-quarter time while hundreds of singers caroled the lyrics. Oma said he felt "terrified and sorely tempted to return on the next ship and never leave Vienna again." While he appreciated the admiration (and the money) received for his performances, he said to Oma that his greatest satisfaction came from the applause of his fellow Viennese. It was really for them that he wrote music.

* * *

YEARS LATER, when I visited exquisite Vienna, I often had the uncanny feeling of knowing what was around the corner or in the next room of places I had never seen. This pre-knowledge, of course, stemmed from earnestly listening to Oma's delightful tales. Oma loved the Viennese scene, and her keen interest in music and the Habsburg royals held her attention. She admired them and brought my 20th-century attention to their bygone lifestyle. I wanted to discover the world that was so normal to them and yet so foreign to me.

The world that Oma knew had changed rapidly, and she bravely kept up while she relished in her memory of the past days. "In Berlin, things are serious but not hopeless. In Vienna, they are hopeless but not serious" (Goodreads, 2023a). Karl Kraus may have had a cynical view of the great city of Vienna, but at least he understood that Vienna could smile. Oma knew this, too.

SPARED NOTHING

PARIS

*O*ma's love for life circled wider than Vienna to include Paris. She enjoyed the *Opera Comique, French cuisine, Offenbach, Haute Couture, Le Can Can,* and the gaiety of West European Vienna. She was also fluent in French and spoke it as a proper *Wiener kind.*

A deep and highly personal tragedy ended Oma's series of happy visits to Paris. She had gone there with a young and attractive cousin, Gabrielle, but tragedy struck while they were in Paris. Oma told me, "Gaby was ever a beautiful mirror of fashion. Her waist was so slender that a man's two hands could easily encircle it." The tragedy is that the excessive corseting had put an enormous strain on her heart, and Oma found her dear cousin dead in her bath. The shock and strain of having the death certified, arrangements to ship Gaby's body back to Vienna, endless forms, and the terrible grief all fell on Oma. She vowed never to return to Paris, where Gaby died. She kept her word and never again visited *La Ville-Lumière.*

For Oma, this incident was a life-changing one. Just as Franz Joseph exclaimed agonizingly after his wife's death: *Mir bleibt auch nichts erspart!* (I am spared nothing). This comment remained engrained in Austrian literal and sardonic *lingua* as a measure of hard times.

It is said that Emperor Franz Joseph uttered these words after a telegram arrived informing him of his beloved wife's assassination. At this point in his life, he already had to endure the loss of a brother and two children to tragic circumstances. It was September 10th, 1898, and the Austrian nation remembered his agonizing words forever: I am spared nothing! Empress Elisabeth had a deep empathy for ordinary people. This characteristic and her outright disregard for aristocratic protocol established her popularity during her lifetime. Austrian society deeply mourned the loss of Empress Sisi with him.

Oma was shocked by the passing of Gaby and mourned her loss deeply while doubts remained about the reason for her death. It could have been a hemorrhage from tuberculosis, but the effects of wasp-waisted tight corsetry at the time could not be ruled out. Joseph Allen Boone points out in an article in the *American Literary History* that whalebone and women carry a contentious history (Boone, 2022):

> Whale baleen also became the mainstay of that other female wardrobe essential of the age, the corset. In contrast to the hooped skirt, there is nothing positive (or healthy) to say about the ribbed corset: Its intention was to enhance women's sexual attributes by creating an impossibly pinched waist and pushing the breasts upward to swell the cleavage. The constriction to the lungs impeded women's capacity to inhale deeply, with deleterious effects on the wearer's energy and health. Corsets were generally fronted with a piece of solid whalebone called the busk, which flattened the belly and accentuated the breasts and hips in contrast (para. 7).

The corset (Universal Group North America LLC/Alamy).

It has been noted that the corset worn by Empress Elisabeth during her assassination enabled her to keep walking to the ferry that she intended to board. The corset was so tightly laced up that it restricted the blood flow. Even though the stabbing wound penetrated her heart directly, the body only delivered a delayed response when it was unlaced, and she succumbed on the boat.

Today, tight-lacing remains a controversial topic. A lengthy discussion on *CorsetMaster* (2020) evokes conflicting perceptions. Some women believe wearing a corset moderately laced without constraining the wearer's health contributes to a feeling of lightness and improved tapering of the female shape. Others argue severe health constrictions are the main reason to condemn corsetry.

Tightly laced bodices have a history from the Middle Ages to the 1960s. With expanding ocean voyages and booming whale fishing industries during the 16th century, the original glue-stiffened bodice curved into a more wearable version made of whale baleen. Whale baleen is more pliable because of its keratinous matter. The material found along the upper jaw of baleen whales sieve the krill and plankton as they feed, and it is thus not a hard bone structure at all. This robust yet flexible medium could be molded into a rigid V-shape that supported the heavy material of the dresses and defined a woman's waist. According to Alexandra Palmer: "When worn, real whalebone becomes soft and pliable from body heat, and the corset comfortably moulds to the torso, making whalebone corsets an expensive luxury" (Palmer, 2021, para. 4).

The name corset, however, only appeared in the early 1800s when it started to dominate western fashion. Lighter girdles appeared in the 1920s, but only after the 1960s did the emphasis shift to a more authentic and realistic focus on health and exercise to maintain a natural figure.

The ecological point of whale hunting to satisfy an aesthetic need brought "whaling as an international industry and the female body as a site of consumption" dangerously close together (Boone, 2022). When lightweight and pliable braces of whalebone replaced the former heavy multiple-layered under-skirts and gave women more freedom of movement, the demand soared until the International Whaling Commission banned the hunting practices in 1955 in the Atlantic and extended the ban globally eleven years later.

Although the corset appeared to be at fault for an array of health problems, death was often caused by other issues. The undergarment may have had an effect, but it cannot bear the sole blame for all the deaths. Some were, in fact, caused by infections or puerperal fever. The arrival of antiseptic techniques changed the statistics. The discovery of tubercle bacillus in 1882 by Robert Koch made it clear that corsets were not the cause of disease. Nor did incidents of breast cancer decrease after corsets changed—as was thought years later—to ones that did not compress the breasts as much as before. After more scientific discoveries, many diseases gradually found alternative explanations for their clinical development unrelated to corset-wearing.

By the mid-1800s, tuberculosis reached epidemic levels in

Europe. People lived in fear of catching the disease with its deadly prognosis. It affected anyone, young and old, male or female, and disregarded class differences. But the worrying thing was that at the time, the disease (also known as consumption) heralded a fashionable association. The fact that the person lost weight and presented a more bleak but rosy-cheeked complexion (while actually wasting away) did not seem to upset them as much. It became fashionable to be unnaturally thin-waisted, pale-faced, and rosy-cheeked. It was even said that beautiful women were more prone to catching the disease... an argument that held no scientific truth or value. But, nearing the end of the century brought lasting change to this misconception (Mullin, 2016):

> The second half of the 19th century ushered in a radically transformed understanding of tuberculosis when, in 1882, Robert Koch announced that he had discovered and isolated the bacteria that caused the disease. By then, germ theory had emerged. This is the idea that microscopic organisms, not miasmas, cause certain diseases. Koch's discovery helped germ theory gain legitimacy and convinced physicians and public health experts that tuberculosis was contagious. Preventing the spread of tuberculosis became the impetus for some of the first large-scale American and European public health campaigns, many of which targeted women's fashions (para. 8,9).

From then on, the long dresses, corsets, and men's lush and luxuriant beards were all targeted as dangerous and possible germ-producing stations. Some scientists and doctors, like Edwin F. Bowers (a doctor who pioneered reflexology in the early 20th century), even went so far as pointing out that "Measles, scarlet fever, diphtheria, tuberculosis, whooping cough, common and uncommon colds, and a host of other infectious diseases can be, and undoubtedly are, transmitted via the whisker route" (Mullin, 2016, para. 13)! But, one thing that the discovery of tubercle bacillus made very clear is that corsets (not too-tightly-laced-in) are not supposed to bear the sole blame for disease.

Yet debate continues blaming the undergarment despite medical facts. Something supposed to support the female structure was later ironically blamed for issues ranging from hysteria to cancer. Although diminishing lung capacity with corset-wearing has been found, mistaken condemnation and correlation of reasons corsets created health issues may have been misinterpreted over the years. Obviously, extreme and unnatural corset tightening to establish a tiny wasp waist was injurious, especially if done with regular use throughout a lifetime. There is no way that the natural bone structure of a human being can withstand any lengthy extreme constraints without changing shape. Corsets may also have affected organ shifting, similar to what happens naturally during pregnancy.

The corset's use declined with the advent of World War I as women could not labor in the fields or factories with such restrictive clothing. Also, household staff who had to work for the war effort left upper-class women of the house to dress without assistance. More comfortable undergarments replaced the corset, but it still took a few decades before the end of the corset era.

SUCH PEOPLE

LIEGNITZ - NEW YORK - NEW JERSEY

*A*lthough Oma occasionally traveled to Berlin, Budapest, Dresden, Salzburg, and the German spas, her heart now lay more with her family at Brucksteine. After Grandfather's death, she found the estate too difficult to manage. "When I sold Brucksteine, I sold part of my heart." Moving to Liegnitz,[1] the grande dame backed several business ventures despite her disdain for "shopkeepers." Some, surprisingly, were successful. Thereupon, naively confident of her business acumen, curiosity prompted her to visit that wild land, America, "where the streets are paved with gold."

Oma's motivations to immigrate to America were probably primarily economic. The Austrian economy was subject to severe stagnation after 1873.[2] By 1900 the clash of polarities between the new and traditional in Austria changed the country forever. This was highly evident in Vienna, which used to be a thriving European metropolis but was suddenly troubled by fears and conflicts. In March 1902, Oma and my mother arrived in New York—two first-class passengers on the deck of a Cunarder. She later recounted, ruefully, how terrified she was at the prospect of encountering "war canoes filled with painted, howling Indians as the ship steamed up New York Bay."

* * *

ONLY AFTER 1818 did cruise ships truly consider the comfort of their passengers. A trip between the UK and the US took three weeks. The Cunard Line has an interesting history that stretches over many years. It started in 1840, and the business was officially called the Cunard Line 38 years later. It was the first steamship company that regularly sailed with transatlantic traffic carrying passengers, founded by Canadian Samuel Cunard. The company continued to enhance the passenger experience by providing a deck where passengers could participate in recreational activities and hide from inclement weather. Before that, passengers had to endure hardship on the journey by sleeping anywhere they could find space in the hold, and they had to provide their own food for the journey.

The Cunard Line had intense competition from the Hamburg-America Line after the 1900s when Germany dominated the transatlantic passenger cruises with their luxurious ships. After the ill-fated Titanic sank in 1912, the Cunard Line bought its struggling company—the White Star—which could never recover after the tragedy. The White Star became part of the Cunard Line, setting the pace for the glamorous days of cruise liner ships after 1920. It became officially known as Cunard White Star, Ltd. in 1934. Many immigrants arrived from Europe at Ellis Island before disembarking on American shores after their long journeys.

After these lengthy ocean voyages, arrival at Ellis Island required more patience. The island may be a tiny spot in the Harbor. Still, it became a symbol of the American Dream after welcoming more than 12 million immigrants throughout its history to American shores. Rising instability, economic hardships, and persecution in Europe started the first immigration wave that hit Ellis Island in the late 1800s. Between 1855 and 1890, almost eight million immigrants arrived from northern Europe through its gates to find solace on new shores. Ellis Island is now a monument to this American story.

On arrival, the passengers had to undergo a lengthy inspection before proceeding to New York City. First- and second-class passengers such as Oma and my mother, Cresentia, avoided this inspection as they were considered to have the means to pay for the journey, which implied a higher level of qualification, affluence, and health. If they showed any medical or legal issues, they were grouped with the third-class passengers (or, as they were known, the steerage section passengers on board) to wait at Ellis Island for an inspection before their arrival on American soil. If an immigrant's papers were in order, it could take up to five hours in the Great Hall before they were allowed to go.

Others were not so lucky and were often detained on the premises for weeks while their documents were inspected and health issues checked. However, the island did receive the moniker "Island of Tears" for those who faced lengthier inspections and challenges on arrival. When Oma and my mother arrived, the island received peak numbers of immigrants from Europe. Many stories lace its history with a "human stream that pours from the steerage of every steamship that docks there, into that huge reservoir, Ellis Island" (Gjenvick-Gjønvik Archives, 2023). In 1954 the island was officially closed when most countries' embassies took over the immigration process. It is said that almost 40% of Americans can trace some ancestry line coming through the gates of Ellis Island.

Immigrants arriving at Ellis Island in 1910 (The New York Public Library).

* * *

As her steamer passed through quarantine and entered New York Harbor, Oma went on deck to catch her first glimpse of this new land. She recalled two vivid memories of the event: She found it difficult to conceive that buildings could be higher than five stories, so she thought the multistoried buildings were built on a series of hills. The other memory was less pleasant. From the deck, Oma and my mother were shown the sights by a stranger when she was called away by the purser. Her handbag with its's important papers, passport, and other valuables lay on her deck chair. Taking my mother with her, she left her bag with a stranger. Needless to say, upon returning, both the handbag and the stranger had vanished. I asked Oma, "Why didn't you take the bag with you?" "Take it with me? That would have been an insult! It would be like calling the man a thief!" Then, she said, the abrupt realization came to her that she was indeed in a new and strange world.

* * *

THE MOST SIGNIFICANT number of immigrants from western and northern Europe arrived in the US after 1870 (more than seven million people). By 1910, almost 70% of immigrants had entered the US from Europe. By the turn of the century, more European immigrants (around three million) arrived from eastern and southern territories, becoming an important factor in American demographics. Immigrants from Europe far outnumbered the ones from other parts of the world, indicating the European need for change and the willingness to face the challenges accompanying these drastic changes. Colonial trade routes had opened up the seaways, and even though these journeys were slow and lengthy, people found new hope for an improved destination that lured them away from their troubles. World War I and World War II slowed down the immigration trends, and it plummeted again during the great depression after the 1920s, but it resumed drastically between these periods.

Poverty and the search for religious freedom (mostly from eastern Europe) prompted immigration to the US. Severe post-war food shortages and the drive for improved economic and social status were additional factors that contributed to this massive global reshuffling. Most of these immigrants were German-speaking from various ethnic backgrounds. Henry Gannet writes the 1900 US census established that approximately 10.4 million of the 76.3 million US inhabitants were born outside America, and more than two million were German-born immigrants (Gannet, 2009).

America became the "Promised Land" despite the hardships endured *en route* and on arrival for some communities. Italian communities, for example, were targeted in New York by crime syndicates, as were German-speaking people after World War I. German schools coexisted with English language schools in the US around 1910, a whopping 554 newspapers were German-oriented, and German-speaking people were fully integrated with American society before the first world war. However, at the outbreak of the war, a new "anti-German hysteria" created suspicion because local people feared their loyalty to the German Emperor and their ethnic-German roots. (Germany was a prominent opponent of the US during the war.) Anti-German sentiment started brewing, creating a rift between Anglo-Americans and Ethnic-Germans. Apart from removing anything "German-like" to protect themselves, the German-speaking population gradually assimilated their cultural habits to conform; they changed their names and only spoke German in their homes.

Most of the settlements started in the northeastern parts of the New York City and Boston areas and then spread southward and westward. Immigrants preferred to maintain unity by living near each other in well-defined ethnic areas.

Over two million Jews arrived after 1880, and their persecution in Europe became more pronounced after the assassination of Czar Alexander II. Their residency, occupational, and educational mobility was severely restricted in Europe, forcing them to move and flee their home countries. The Russo-Japanese war (1904) threatened their safety, and most fled from forced conscription. Most of these Jewish immigrants found refuge in the US and settled in New York's Lower East Side to avoid being used as human barriers to "stop Japanese bullets" in Manchuria in northeast China.

KLEINDEUTSCHLAND, ALSO KNOWN AS "LITTLE GERMANY," was the largest German-American neighborhood in Manhattan, New York City, by 1845, and its German inhabitants showed a rapid growth in population density by 1860. The German-speaking community tended to group together more than others and even preferred to remain in their close-knit home-country groups—especially the Prussians.

They also differed from other immigrant nationalities by their skill sets and education levels; many German immigrants were cabinet makers or in the construction industry. Well-known people like Friedrich Sorge and Oswald Ottendorfer hailed from this area and engaged in the political world and trade unions. Ottendorfer was the socially prominent owner-editor of the *Staatszeitung*, which was the largest newspaper in the German language. The area was a flourishing German cultural hub, and only Vienna and Berlin had more German-speaking inhabitants during the final years before the 20th century.

Tompkins Square Park was at the center, and the bustling community established its traditional social structures to support the inhabitants in the new world abroad. There were beer halls, oyster saloons, theaters, social meeting places, clubs, businesses with typical German appeal, reading rooms and libraries, German churches, synagogues, schools, and German newspapers. Architects played a significant role in its design, and small two or three-story houses lining the streets were subdivided to accommodate all the families. Around the turn of the century, many Germans moved out of East Village to make room for the increasing new immigrant flow comprised mainly of Jewish descent.

An unfortunate incident that added to the German exodus from *Kleindeutschland* occurred on June 15, 1904, when a paddle-wheeler named *General Slocum* set out on the East River with a large group of women and children. They planned to have a picnic on Long Island, but shortly after departure, the boat caught fire, and due to inadequate safety equipment and sub-standard navigation captaincy, the boat sank, and 1,021 passengers on board died. This incident rocked the German community as many of the deceased were prominent members of their society and established families that were the foundation of *Kleindeutschland*. Together with the influx of other nationalities and increasing anti-German sentiment fueled by World War I, this disaster eventually led to the extinction of Little Germany. The area gradually changed into the Lower East Side, with the addition of Irish, Russian, and Yiddish-speaking immigrants from Eastern Europe and Southern Italy after 1880, hence losing its typical uniform character and changing rapidly into a more cosmopolitan neighborhood as the German population moved elsewhere.

* * *

OMA and my mother lived in Hoboken, New Jersey, a large German-speaking population center outside New York City. This is where my mother spied her future husband in a Hoboken laundry, telling Oma, "I just saw a man, and if he asks me to marry him, I will." Oma was dumbstruck when my father asked for her daughter's hand one day. "If you take my daughter from me, who," she asked, "will fix my hair? I have never done it myself." Thereafter, to her dying day, she wore dainty dust caps to cover her ignorance of the art of coiffure. When she wished to appear in public (or on occasions where the dust cap was unsuitable), Oma summoned a hairdresser. But sometimes, these good women were unable to leave their salons.

Fortunately, Madam Margarete Matzenauer—the Hungarian mezzo-soprano—was a friend from Vienna and an American neighbor. The diva knew something of the fundamentals of hair styling and was able to fill in for the professionals. During the course of several of my visits, "Matzenauer" (as Oma called her) performed the rites of coiffure. The two spoke animated Hungarian, of which I knew not a single word. In return for her favors, Oma religiously attended every Matzenauer performance, and when my visits coincided with these events, I was taken in tow and told when to applaud. After the opera, we would meet for champagne—and chocolate for me—in her dressing room.

"Matzenauer" (INTERFOTO/Alamy).

Madam Matzenauer (1881–1963) could do more than style hair. With her wide opulent range in her mezzo-soprano voice, she performed some of the most important operatic works from German and Italian composers in Europe as well as America, including 19 seasons at the Met, an appearance at The Royal Albert Hall, and a role in Columbia Pictures as Madame Pomponi of the production, *Mr. Deeds Goes to Town*.

She was born to a musical family in Temesvár, Austria-Hungary (now known as Timișoara in Românía). She was a Hungarian of Jewish descent. She married an Italian tenor, Edoardo Ferrari-Fontana, but sadly, the marriage ended in divorce a few years later. She had a brilliant repertoire and left a beautiful legacy as an opera singer with major roles in Il Trovatore, Carmen, Aida, and Wagner's Tristan und Isolde. In her later years, she started teaching, and two of her pupils became prominent mezzo-sopranos.

* * *

IN DUE COURSE, I entered the world. When the day neared to enter elementary school, Oma had the first of a series of head-on collisions with the American system of education in a small rural community. She requested, via a hand-delivered letter, that she be granted an interview with the local superintendent of education. Since my father was an important taxpayer and had written the request in English, the appointment was promptly arranged.

At the appointed hour, Oma swept into the unsuspecting superintendent's office and announced that the interview would be conducted in French. Although she spoke French, German, Czech, Polish, and Hungarian, the syntax and pronunciation of English eluded her almost completely; hence the suggested French interview was obviously defensive.

The superintendent protested that he did not speak French, and she went through her catalog of languages, carefully omitting English. But every time, the poor man simply responded, "but I don't know that language." Finding no mutual conversational medium, she made a grand exit. Once within the safety of the family circle, she demanded to know, "How can such people be expected to educate my grandson?"

There were later interviews. Mother was once dragooned to accompany Oma in the role of interpreter. With the stiff opening amenities over, Oma asked the superintendent, "At what age will my grandson begin counterpoint." The reply was, "We do not teach sewing to the boys." The interview was terminated then and there.

The superintendent Oma met was likely a contemporary of
David D. Taylor, the Principal at Marlborough High School
(The Pioneer of the Marlborough High School).

Her opinion of American education plummeted to a new low.

COUNTERPOINT IS a musical term describing the functional independence of various voices that create one harmonious and complete composition. Perhaps it is most clearly explained this way (Counterpoint, 2020):

These voices, losing independence, are fused into one, and the parallel chords are perceived as single tones with a new timbre. This effect is also used in orchestral arrangements; for instance, in Ravel's *Bolero #5*, the parallel part of the flutes, horn, and celesta resemble the sound of an electric organ. In counterpoint, parallel voices are prohibited because they violate the homogeneity of musical texture when independent voices occasionally disappear, turning into a new timbre quality and vice versa (para. 7).

The harmony of two lines or voices is interdependent in counterpoint, while the melodic structure and rhythm remain dependent on each other. The term translates from Latin, *punctus contra punctum*: point against point. It was developed and used during the Classical, Renaissance, and Baroque music eras. An easily understandable example of this complex term is to sing the songs *Frère Jacques* and *Three Blind Mice* together. They are independent melodies but create a harmonically interdependent composition when joined. There are a number of well-known songs that share this progression.

* * *

THE BENDING of the twig continued. I was enrolled in the first grade, and the great day to begin school arrived. The usual tears, head patting, and advice from all quarters accompanied my launching into the academic world.

I was sent home on the second day for "being fresh." When questioned about this by my dumbfounded parents, my father broke out in a broad grin: "You answered the teacher in a mixture of three languages. She thought you were showing off by speaking in English, French, and German." I protested that I do the same thing at home, and nobody thinks I am "being fresh." "What are languages?" I asked them. This was my first realization that thoughts are conveyed by more than mere words. I then understood that words must be selected and employed within a certain context of something called a language. Needless to say, my dear Oma triumphantly responded, upon hearing of my trilingual *faux pas* "How can such people teach my grandson?"

Marlboro Public School (Courtesy of the McCourt
Collection).

Oma had difficulty not only with English but also with the
concept of democracy. She was puzzled at the English singular
and plural use of "you." "In German, one addresses servants and
family members with the familiar form (du). The formal 'sie' is
used in addressing strangers of equal station, casual acquain-
tances, and superiors.

The third person singular (and first person plural) is
employed only in extremely formal situations." Thus, Oma was
constantly at a loss to know the exact social status of those with
whom she came in contact.

* * *

ARRANGEMENTS WERE MADE for regular visits to Oma during
school holidays, and I would dream for weeks about the preparations. I dreamed about the stories she would tell me, the delicacies she would provide, and the amusements awaiting me.
Aristocrats ate five times a day, and Oma followed suit!

Young boys are known for their insatiable appetites; mine
was no different. The parade of meals at Oma's made a deep and

lasting impression. Mornings arrived with a small cup of mocha and a sweet roll. At 10 a.m., a second breakfast was served in the form of fresh *Kaisersemmel* rolls, fruit, pastry, and coffee.

Kaisersemmel rolls are particularly hard-fermented round rolls made from wheat with a distinguishing five-segmented pinwheel cut or fold on the top that represents a crown. They have a crispy texture outside with a soft dough interior. These rolls originated in Austria and became famous during the 1760s. They were most probably named after Emperor Franz Joseph, although some sources believe that the name is derived from a specific baker during the 1800s by the name of Kayser. It was known as a luxurious product due to its laborious production. The preparation requires multiple rising sessions and a particular folding that demands some skillful practice.

Luncheon was a more formal affair with soup, an *entrée*, fruit, dessert—of course, with whipped cream—and coffee. Mid-afternoon provided another *snackl*[3] to keep me going until dinner at seven. The main meal of the day usually consisted of favorites of mine: Viennese chicken basted in butter, essential vegetables, and truly marvelous pastries. And when I was permitted to stay up later, a night-time snackl completed the day's glorious culinary intake.

By contrast, at home, I only had three regular meals per day with occasional snacks. When I asked Oma once why we ate so much at her house, she replied, "It is absolutely barbarous to subject your digestive system to a sudden avalanche of food. Besides, it is pleasant to sit down occasionally and talk; food should be incidental to the conversation."

* * *

AUSTRIAN COURT TRADITIONS were highly sophisticated and regulated by strict protocol. Even though it is said that Emperor Franz Joseph had modest culinary demands, the rest of his court (as well as the staff) had to be fed, and high standards prevailed. This could be said for any imperial family in Europe at the time. Specific time was set aside for family interaction, and this was usually accompanied by some kind of nutritious fare. According to the records, if family members were invited to a dinner, they were obliged to attend. They could only be excused if they provided a trustworthy medical reason for their absence. So, it was taken seriously to feast and socialize together.

The days started early for these preparations in the Hofburg court kitchen, usually at five in the morning. The kitchen was divided into sections: The *Hofzehrgaden* was responsible for purchasing and storing food; the *Hofzuckerbächkerei* was the "confectionary" department responsible for drinks, sweetmeats, and frozen foods; while the *Hofkeller* was the cellar department. Since most of the meals were eaten at the place of work due to the absence of a canteen, it took almost two hours to distribute lunch at the Hofburg court to the more than 2000 employees! The *Kaisermenü* (traditional Viennese fare) was, of course, the best quality of the day and was eaten at midday by the Emperor himself. His meal usually consisted of a three-course meal starting with soup, meat with a side dish, and a pastry as dessert. Evening meals at court were mostly smoked fish, cold meats, or sausage with vegetables and bread, served with wine or beer.

Apart from the lavish food at the imperial palace, the other Austrian-Hungarian hierarchical classes also exhibited a gastronomic fondness for quality food. Some of these dishes have prevailed since then. Dishes like the *Wiener Schnitzel* (which actually originated from Italy but was brought to Vienna by a Czech general) are still world famous. At the time, food preservation was mainly done through salt and ice. No freezers were available. Only during the Napoleonic wars did canned food (in glass containers) become more well-known and change the gastronomic menu forever. Until then, everything was freshly planned and prepared. Potatoes were widespread and made the staple meals for many families, regardless of their social status. Austrian cooking is known for being one of the most varied in Europe, including traces from Italy, Czechoslovakia, Hungary, and Germany. The cultural mix of northern European food developed and mingled to such an extent that even nowadays, one finds a Hungarian *goulash* or an Austrian *apfelstrudel* in adjacent countries just as they were made in Oma's time. And the key to the quality remains a well-prepared meal with fresh ingredients.

The Austrian coffee house is another well-known institution that prevailed from the earlier centuries. These institutions were distinctly part of the Austrian way of life with a particular atmosphere, and they established places for meeting people while having a light breakfast, light lunch, or even just a snack. Even today, it has become part of a lifestyle for city dwellers to have a mid-afternoon break at one of these immaculate coffee houses in Europe. Many of these coffee houses were also famous meeting places for writers and poets who exchanged their craft via live readings and general gatherings.

At Oma's house, we had a similar array of quality meals with accompanying conversations while lounging around the table. My pre-Christmas visits were especially memorable. A regular highlight was the matinee performance of Hansel and Gretel at the old Metropolitan Opera House, followed by dinner at Lüchow's, located at East 14th Street, which was by far Oma's favorite restaurant in the new world.

* * *

HANSEL AND GRETEL, conducted by Richard Strauss at the Metropolitan, had been one of the most popular Christmas season opera performances since its performance in the Hoftheater in Weimar, Germany, in 1893. After its initial performance, it appeared abroad, with the first American production in New York in 1895. The fairy-tale opera was composed by Engelbert Humperdinck, the famous 19th-century composer, based on the Brothers Grimm's famous fairy tale. The production remained a festive holiday tradition that resonated well with children and adults throughout its stage career—spanning many decades. It remains one of the most successful operas that was ever created.

The German composer Engelbert Humperdinck (1854–1921) was an assistant to Richard Wagner, and Hansel and Gretel was his first opera that framed his musical reputation for the rest of his life. The opera was a huge success, and the folk tale of the two lost children encountering the wicked witch in the woods revolutionized the immense impact of the Brothers Grimm's academic influence on the understanding of linguistic development at the time. Over the years, the Met orchestra maintained its excellence with the lightness of its folk-inspired musical score.

* * *

UNFORTUNATELY, the building where Lüchow's was situated burned down in the early 1990s under suspicious circumstances. It used to be the only place to see and be seen in the area around the turn of the previous century. East 14th Street, Manhattan, New York City, looked completely different in the late 19th century with entertainment places like the city's opera house, the Academy of Music, and the City Theater movie house. At the heart of these artistic ventures was the meeting place for musicians and the literary crowd, where quality dining and live music used to complete a night out. At the same time, it catered to the extensive German population of East Village. The restaurant served typical high-quality German food consisting of a beer garden, a men's grill, seven separate dining rooms, and a bar. Here, the German population could enjoy their wiener schnitzel, among other traditional fares. And, of course, the place was famous for its excellent beer.

It is said that the restaurant owes its inception to the piano magnate and famous German immigrant William Steinway who became known as the "patron saint of Lüchow's." He granted a loan to a former waiter and German immigrant, August Lüchow, to establish the restaurant in the city's most prestigious area where Steinway's friends and musicians from all over the world assembled to entertain and be entertained. Some of the most celebrated people who entered the Lüchow's doors over a century of its existence were famous conductor Leonard Bernstein, actress and singer Marlene Dietrich, Czech composer Antonïn Dvořák, the prima Russian ballerina Anna Pavlova, and even the 26th president of the US Theodore Roosevelt—among many other famous personas. The world-famous composer, Victor Herbert, conducted an eight-piece Viennese orchestra at the establishment until its demise.

DUE TO CHANGING German sentiment induced by politics and global wars, the *umlaut* in the name was often dropped and reinstated according to changing times. However, this did not affect the food quality or the venue's ambiance! After its establishment in 1882, it remained a prominent landmark, with frequent ownership changes during the 1950s to 1980s, never recovering its former glory. In 1995, the building was demolished, and only the memory of a lost era remained ingrained in local society. Most other buildings in the block were also changed, replaced with newer ones, or completely demolished, and the whole street took on a new character.

* * *

Lüchow's (Chronicle / Alamy).

OMA WAS KNOWN to the staff and greeted deferentially by name and elaborate ceremony. She had her special table in the corner, below the orchestra platform, and the conductor would nod a greeting and send a waiter to obtain a select list of requests that Oma would want to hear. As an adult, I often visited Lüchow's, sat at her table whenever possible, and reminisced of a time long ago when the boy I once was dined there with his beloved Oma.

Aside from the opera, meals at home, and Lüchow's, Oma made other arrangements for my amusement. I usually elected to go to Coney Island. Oma herself never accompanied me. She sent a servant along who was amply supplied with funds for candied apples, pink lemonade, rides, and other things so important to young boys.

Returning home to the routine life in a small country village required something of an adjustment. My opera-going was kept a deep secret from my peers, who looked suspiciously at anyone who liked to hear women sing opera! It was always good to see my parents again, but I would begin immediately to dream of my next visit to Oma.

* * *

OMA LIVED LONG ENOUGH to see the way of life she knew and loved collapse and vanish. The crowning insult, in her eyes, was the rise of an obscure Austrian painter to power even greater than that held by her beloved Franz Josef.

Now they are all gone. Oma, grandfather, mother, and her two brothers. Brucksteine itself lies deep and inaccessible behind the Iron Curtain in Southern Poland.

Oma lived a long life, long enough to see the way of life familiar to her collapse and vanish. Brucksteine became a nostalgic memory.

Oma must be happy if, at last, she is again in the company of Strauss, Brahms, and perhaps her irascible old friend, Smetana. Heaven would be heaven indeed for her if the angelic hosts were occasionally to sing in three-quarter time. Knowing her, perhaps she has arranged it.

FIN

EPILOGUE

*A*ccording to *Patterns of Growth and Stagnation in the Late Nineteenth Century Habsburg Economy* (Schulze, 2000), three factors affected the Austrian economic decline:

Austria *per capita* income failed to expand at a pace broadly commensurate with the country's relative income position. The Austrian economy did not catch up with the leaders and failed to keep pace with other "followers." Second, the Hungarian economy recorded a markedly higher rate of *per capita* income growth, placing it about mid-range in a European growth comparison. Third, the new evidence supports the notion of a "great depression" in the western half of the empire (Austria) after 1873. The distinct periodicity and differential rates of Austrian and Hungarian growth are consistent with the argument that the outflow of Austrian capital to Hungary after the 1873 Vienna stock market crash was crucial in prolonging economic stagnation in Austria, whilst fueling the widespread wave of industrialization in Hungary. The reversal of this capital outflow in the early 1890s was associated with an increase in Austrian economic growth and a decrease in Hungary's rate of expansion.

The capital flow between Austria and Hungary most probably affected the Zimmerman family fortune. The 1873 Vienna market crash occurred when Oma was seventeen, then most likely married to Anton. The notion of a great—and long—depression in Lower Silesia spanning until the Austrian economic growth of the 1890s is remarkable. The tide turned economically in her mid-thirties. When she was widowed is unknown. Given the age disparity of husband and wife, she was most certainly widowed during the post-1873 great depression, which would have prompted the sale of that piece of her heart known as Brucksteine. It would follow that the business successes she enjoyed in Liegnitz may have occurred in the 1890s when the Austrian economy improved. Following her immigration in 1902, Oma opened and financed a bakery in New City and Congers, New York, but lived in Hoboken, New Jersey—in commuting distance to the Metropolitan Opera in order to to see Madam Matzenauer. She was said to have been living with a Jewish man in her later years. It is unknown how this presumed union impacted her economic status.

With the cultured life Oma led in Europe, her interest in immigrating to New York in 1902 was not, perhaps, solely economic but motivated by the political climate. Had Oma stayed to the final gasps of the Austro-Hungarian Empire, she would have seen Lower Silesia become part of the changing German empire. Minority groups from Lower Silesia—and Germany—experienced an "ethnic preoccupation and the decline of liberalism" during 1898–1933. Silesians fought for German national unification and Jewish emancipation (Kurlander, 2002), though with traces of anti-Semitism. Before this decline of liberalism, Lower Silesia and Schleswig Holstein provinces were considered the most liberal-thinking.

The newly established Austrian republic had shrunk to about one-fourth of the former Austro-Hungarian Empire. Although the country contained a host of ethnic groups and minority groups, the German population sector remained the strongest and identified strongly with German nationalism.[1] Had Oma not immigrated to New York and remained in Lower Silesia, she would have been among these "ethnic Germans"— regardless of her country of origin, a legacy of a defunct Empire.

Had she stayed, she would have witnessed a Vienna faced with many problems following World War I: one-third of its population was concentrated in Vienna. Significant housing shortages abounded after population growth and housing construction no longer matched the needed expansion. The city also opened its doors to war refugees, and high post-war rentals exasperated the housing issue further. Vienna became over-crowded, and the economy struggled.

* * *

IT WAS NOT JUST Brucksteine that remained behind the Iron Curtain. Her sons Hans and August remained, except for a few U.S. visits before World War II. They were stuck in East Germany.

The Iron Curtain became the term used for a geo-politically defining barrier between East and West after World War II. Winston Churchill coined the metaphor in his famous speech at Westminster College in Fulton, Missouri on March 5, 1946 (Westminster College, 2019):

> From Stettin in the Baltic to Trieste in the Adriatic an 'iron curtain' has descended across the continent. Behind that line lie all the capitals of the ancient states of Central and Eastern Europe. Warsaw, Berlin, Prague, Vienna, Budapest, Belgrade

Bucharest and Sofia; all these famous cities and the populations around them lie in what I must call the Soviet sphere, and all are subject, in one form or another, not only to Soviet influence but to a very high and in some cases increasing measure of control from Moscow (para. 2).

These words also traced back to events in Europe before the Second World War, including the 1917 Russian Revolutions and their annexations of Eastern European nations. After World War II, the individual military alliances of the Warsaw Pact and the North Atlantic Treaty Organization functioned as opposing international military and economic alliances until the Berlin Wall finally came down in 1989.

Crescentia, Oma, and Hans, in 1939 at Crescentia's home in Marlborough, New York. Hans and August visited the U.S. before World War II (Courtesy of the McCourt Collection).

GLOSSARY

Ancien Régime: The political and social ruling system before the French Revolution in 1789. It translates as "old order" from French and implies that everyone was the King of France's subject and belonged to a specific "estate." The latter was divided into three orders: the clergy, nobility, and the Third Estate. At the time, no national citizenship existed.

Apfelstrudel: Apple strudel is a typical oblong and sweet Austrian pastry consisting mainly of dough and apples. The word strudel is Middle High German, meaning "swirl" or "whirlpool." Today, it is still a popular pastry in the surrounding areas and especially in the countries that formerly belonged to the Habsburg Empire. Strudel traditionally derives from Vienna; the oldest known recipe dates back to 1697.

Arpeggio: A sequence of notes of a musical chord played in rapid ascending or descending succession. It may span more than one octave.

Bit schlag: *Schlag* is the German word for whipped cream. The word *bit* means a little. The two words are used conjunctively as an expression for a little whipped cream, especially when topped on the cake.

Bleigiessen: The word translates as "lead pouring." It is practiced as a New Year's Eve tradition in Germany and some northern European countries. It involves melting a piece of lead poured into cold water to establish a shape that is then interpreted as a prediction.

Brioche: A light bread that tastes slightly sweet and has a yeasty dough consistency. It is similar to the *croissant*. The word's first known use was in 1826, which can be traced back to Austria and France. Its shapes differ depending on where it's found. In Italy, it takes the familiar crescent shape of the *croissant* with a more crispy texture, while in other countries, the shape is round and more "doughy."

(Le) Can Can: A typical dance form originating from France that involves high kicking and swirling of a dress and ruffled petticoats to expose the woman's legs and sometimes more. It is often associated with fast and dizzying dances, and the word was used for the first time in 1830.

Coiffure: Hairstyle: A way of styling and arranging the woman's hair. The word is borrowed from the French verb *coiffer*, meaning to cover or arrange.

Croissant: A crescent-shaped flaky pastry with a slightly sweet taste. The word originates from Middle French. The name was used for the first time in 1875, and its etymology is based on the present participle of the word "to grow" (*croistre*) in French and *crescere* in Latin. The delightful pastry is world-famous and hails from France.

Demi-monde: Class of women who were considered to be of dubious moral nature and social standing.

Du: The German direct address of "you" in the singular form (the plural form is *ihr*). *Du* is mainly used on a familiar basis when addressing someone. (As opposed to *sie*.)

Eclat: In the 17th century, the word éclat literally "burst" into language, meaning an ostentatious display, mostly publicly.

It is derived from the French meaning "splinter" or "burst." In Old French, the word was originally *esclat*. The word (and its use in idiom form: to make an éclat) generally implies a sensational creation, acclamation, or lavish applause.

Entrée: The word's etymology derives from French, with its first use in 1692. It has three implicit meanings: A first course of a meal, having the freedom to enter, or making an entrance. The culinary connotation of the word is traced back to England in the 18th century when formal dinners required more than one course with impressive side dishes. An entrée dish was a smaller version or side dish but a very important part of introducing the centerpiece dish, like the meat or fish. Because the word has such an elegant ring to it, the use of it remained an important culinary part of serving an array of dishes to impress.

French cuisine: France's indigenous cooking style and traditions are called *Cuisine française*. It has been influenced and developed through many dishes from the surrounding European areas. In the 20th century, *Guide Michelin* and culinary tourism enhanced its development and high standard while promoting bourgeois culinary delights to the commoner people. French cuisine often consists of three courses, namely the *entrée* (also *hors d'oeuvre*) followed by the main course and completed with a cheese course or dessert.

Faux pas: A beautiful description of an embarrassing "blunder." It can also indicate an improper remark, socially unacceptable word, or sentence. It is derived from French, with the first use in 1676.

Gesinde: The word has Germanic roots; in old German, it translates as a follower. In Dutch, the word *gezin*, meaning family, is related to the Germanic word. **Hofgesinde** was related to noble homes.

Goulash: A typical red meat and vegetable stew with a distinctive paprika-seasoned flavor originating from Hungary, a national dish symbolic of Hungarian culture. It was a hearty meal for commoners, and its origins trace back to the 10th century when it was eaten by shepherds. The word is based on the Hungarian *gulya*, which means "herd of cattle," and the noun *gulyás*, meaning herdsman. It is still predominantly served and enjoyed in central parts of Europe.

Grande Armée: The largest European assembled military component during the French Emperor Napoleon's reign. The soldiers were sent to combat Russia, and the force comprised about 500,000 soldiers, including staff members responsible for directly reporting to Napoleon.

Grande dame: An elegant older lady with prestige and abilities. It is literally translated from the French as "great lady."

Haute Couture: The noun is derived from French and translates as "high sewing," which means exclusive and mostly trend-setting fashions designed by specific designers and design houses. The most popular names that fall under *Haute Couture* are Chanel, Gucci, Christian Dior, and Armani, to name a few.

Herrschaftshaus: A manor house or stately home in German.

Höhere Mädchenschule: Schools of higher education for girls in German-speaking countries. It was mainly intended for girls of the wealthy bourgeoisie and aimed to prepare them to become wives and mothers by teaching them appropriate social graces and rites of etiquette.

Hofkeller: The cellar of a noble home.

Hofzehrgaden: The people in charge of purchasing and storing food for the noble home.

Hofzuckerbächkerei: The "confectionary" department responsible for drinks, sweetmeats, and frozen foods of the noble home.

Iron Curtain: A geo-politically defining barrier between East and West after World War II. Winston Churchill coined the metaphor.

Kaisermenü: The typical traditional Viennese fare and culinary delights of the elite.

Kaisersemmel: This is a yeast bread roll made from white bread flour, sometimes called a "bulkie" in Boston, U.S. The bread has a typical pinwheel-shaped cut on top with a firm and crispy crust and a soft and moist texture inside. They are large and round, originating from Austria in the 15th century.

Kipfel: The word is a diminutive of the German *kipf* or Old High German *kipfa*, which means wagon post. It is a firm biscuit of bread with a typical crescent shape (much like a *croissant*).

Kleindeutschland: Formerly, Little Germany in New York's Lower East Side.

Knödel: A German word meaning dumpling. It is sometimes also known as knoedel. The dumpling's etymology hails from Middle High German and Old High German *knodo*. It is a diminutive of the word *knode*, which means knot.

Krapfen: This dough delight is filled with jam or custard, dusted with sugar, and is mainly known as a doughnut. Krapfen was probably the first European doughnut-style pastry. The dough is leavened and then deep-fried to create a soft, moist, and airy texture with a sweet taste. It is a typical sweet Austrian pastry and is world-famous! Over the years, many varieties have evolved, and they are enjoyed especially during festive seasons in different cultures.

La Ville Lumière: The City of Lights, also known as Paris, France.

Loge: A small partitioned booth or compartment in a theater or at the entrance of a building. In a theater, it can be part of a section with raised seats for improved viewing. The use of the word goes back to 1749, with its origins in Old French, meaning a shelter.

Mädchenpensionat: Wealthy families sent their girls to "finishing" schools of a slightly higher standard than *Mädchenschule* or *Töchterschule*.

"**Mir bleibt auch nichts erspart**": I am spared nothing. These are the memorable words uttered by Franz Joseph when he received the news of the assassination of his beloved wife, Empress Elisabeth. His life was filled with unfortunate events, and as a result, the famous sentence became a linguistic exclamation in the Austrian lingua to express misfortune.

Modiste: A person who makes and sells fashion items like dresses or hats for women, from the French word *mode* meaning style.

Molybdomancy: Another name for the age-old tradition of lead-pouring. It is often associated with folk medicine and fortune-telling or superstition.

Objets d'art: These are articles of artistic value, sometimes called curios. The phrase originates from French and translates as "art objects." It's a phrase that accompanies objects derived from different cultures and places while traveling.

Offenbach: Jacques Offenbach was a Jewish cellist and French composer of German descent who lived from 1819–1880. He was generally known as "der Offenbacher" and is famous for his 100 operettas composed over 20 years after 1850. He was a strong influence on Johann Strauss II. His first famous operetta is called *Orphée aux Enfers* (Orpheus in the Underworld), which remains one of his most often performed operettas. He was granted the Légion d'Honneur by Napoleon III.

Opéra Comique: In French, it literally means "comic opera," but it implies a theater production interspersed with operatic arias. Spoken dialogue between the arias completes the wholeness of an opéra comique.

Par excellence: An adjective indicating that something is the best of a kind. It is often associated with physical characteristics, exceptional *cuisine,* architecture, and designs. The word's first known use was in 1695, hailing from the French language.

Per capita: An adjective or adverb defining something equal to individuals, often per unit for each nation, person, or concept. Its etymology hails from Medieval Latin, meaning "by heads." Synonyms for the phrase are "each" or "a piece."

Pince-nez: Glasses or spectacles without earpieces for support. They are worn on the tip of the nose—pinching the nose. Hence the noun is derived from the French words *pincer* (to pinch) and *nez* (nose). The style was very popular during the late 1800s to early 1900s, and a *pince-nez* was often attached to the person's clothes or the ear with a suspension chain because it could easily fall off and get lost. People preferred to use this instead of formal spectacles because, at the time, there was a stigma to wearing permanent glasses.

Ringstrasse: The circular boulevard that embraces the old parts of Vienna. It is known as one of the most beautiful streets in the world. With the boulevard's construction, the Viennese suburbs were connected to the powerhouse of the city's center. Kaiser Franz Joseph realized his dream by authenticating the completion of the street.

Sacher torte: A typical Austrian chocolate cake (*torte*) with a filling of apricot jam. Its etymology hails from the famous German family Sacher, renowned proprietors of Austrian restaurants in the 19th and 20th centuries.

Sie: German address for "you" in the singular and plural but only used in the formal context when addressing a person, primarily when addressing an adult respectfully.

Töchterschule: Similar to *Mädchenschule.*

Umlaut: Diacritical mark of two points over a vowel (e.g., ö, ë, ü). It generally indicates a change in pronunciation with a more pronounced front or central articulation.

Wiener kind: A child of Vienna.

Wiener Edelknaben: A noble boy who serves the Court, also known as a Page.

Wiener schnitzel: This Austrian dish is a famous thin veal cutlet crumbed and fried. Its origins are uncertain, even though it has become known as Vienna's official (albeit unassuming) dish. It is said that the schnitzel may have originated in Italy, where it is called *costoletta alla Milanese.* It is customarily served with potatoes and sliced lemon.

BIBLIOGRAPHY

Albert. (2020, October 13). In *Wikipedia*. https://en.wikipedia.org/wiki/Albert

Allegheny College Pelletier Library. (2009). *The Ida M. Tarbell collection, 1890--1944/prentice-hall, inc.* Allegheny College. https://dspace.allegheny.edu/bitstream/handle/10456/21049/05.1468.0001.pdf?sequence=1&isAllowed=y

Alpine Manager. (2014, December 31). *Bleigiessen (lead pouring) predictions for the new year*. The Alpine Village. https://alpinevillagecenter.com/bleigiessen-lead-pouring-predictions-new-year/

American Duchess. (2012, March 13). V73: a brief history of feathers-on-hats. *American Duchess Blog*. https://blog.americanduchess.com/2012/03/v73-brief-history-of-feathers-on-hats.html

Apple Strudel. (2020, January 28). In *Wikipedia*. https://en.wikipedia.org/wiki/Apple_strudel

Archduke Franz Ferdinand of Austria. (2019, April 20). In *Wikipedia*. https://en.wikipedia.org/wiki/Archduke_Franz_Ferdinand_of_Austria

Austria. (n.d.). *Austria's history*. www.austria.info. https://www.austria.info/en/service-and-facts/about-austria/history

Bethencourt, F. (2007, July). *Black Africans in Renaissance Europe*. Reviews in history. https://reviews.history.ac.uk/review/619

Biographics. (2019). *Franz Josef: The last great emperor*. [Video]. YouTube. https://youtu.be/EtJ2sbVkZGI

Blakeley, A. (1997, May 1). *Problems in studying the role of blacks in europe*. Perspectives on History. https://www.historians.org/research-and-publications/perspectives-on-history/may-1997/problems-in-studying-the-role-of-blacks-in-europe

Blakely, A. (2008, February 9). *The black presence in pre-20th century Europe: a hidden history*. BlackPast. https://www.blackpast.org/global-african-history/black-presence-pre-20th-century-europe-hidden-history/

Bölükbasi, B. (2021, December 30). *Lead pouring: The new year's eve tradition has been banned since 2018 - these are non-toxic alternatives*. The Limited Times. https://newsrnd.com/life/2021-12-30-lead-pouring--the-new-year-s-eve-tradition-has-been-banned-since-2018---these-are-non-toxic-alternatives.S1IidQjst.html

Bonura, M. (2012). Napoleonic memory and the French officer corps: An analysis of le spectateur militaire from 1826 to 1836. *Napoleonica. LaRevue, 15*(3), 106–118. https://www.cairn.info/revue-napoleonica-la-revue-2012-3-page-106.htm?contenu=article

Boone, J. A. (2022). Whalebone, hoop skirts, corsets, pants roles: Women and the Melville effect in contemporary art. *American Literary History*. https://doi.org/10.1093/alh/ajac080

Brinkhoff, T. (n.d.). *Mrokocin (kamieniec ząbkowicki, wałbrzych subregion, Poland) - population statistics, charts, map, location, weather and web information*. City Population. https://www.citypopulation.de/en/poland/localities/walbrzyski/kamieniec_z%C4%85bkowicki/0852654__mrokocin/?

Britannica, T. Editors of Encyclopaedia. (2022, December 10). *Albert, Prince Consort. Encyclopedia Britannica*. https://www.britannica.com/biography/Albert-Prince-Consort

Britannica, T. Editors of Encyclopaedia. (2019). *Ancien régime French history. Encyclopædia Britannica*. https://www.britannica.com/event/ancien-regime

Britannica, T. Editors of Encyclopaedia. (2020). *Bedřich Smetana Bohemian composer. Encyclopædia Britannica*. https://www.britannica.com/biography/Bedrich-Smetana

Britannica, T. Editors of Encyclopaedia. (2011, April 24). *Congress of Troppau Europe [1820]. Encyclopedia Britannica*. https://www.britannica.com/event/Congress-of-Troppau

Britannica, T. Editors of Encyclopaedia. (n.d.). *Esterházy family. Encyclopaedia Britannica*. https://www.britannica.com/topic/Esterhazy-family

Britannica, T. Editors of Encyclopaedia. (n.d.). *Göttingen Germany. Encyclopaedia Britannica*. https://www.britannica.com/place/Gottingen

Britannica, T. Editors of Encyclopaedia. (2018). *Iron Curtain. Encyclopædia Britannica*. https://www.britannica.com/event/Iron-Curtain

Britannica, T. Editors of Encyclopaedia (2020). *Johann Strauss II. Encyclopedia Britannica*. https://www.britannica.com/biography/Johann-Strauss-II

Britannica, T. Editors of Encyclopaedia. (n.d.). *Legnica Poland. Encyclopaedia Britannica*. https://www.britannica.com/place/Legnica

Britannica, T. Editors of Encyclopaedia. (n.d.). *Maximilian archduke of Austria and emperor of Mexico. Encyclopædia Britannica*. https://www.britannica.com/biography/Maximilian-archduke-of-Austria-and-emperor-of-Mexico

Britannica, T. Editors of Encyclopaedia. (2019). *The Moldau symphonic poem by Smetana. Encyclopædia Britannica*. https://www.britannica.com/topic/The-Moldau

Britannica, T. Editors of Encyclopaedia. (n.d.). *Napoleonic wars - the retreat from Moscow. Encyclopedia Britannica*. https://www.britannica.com/event/Napoleonic-Wars/The-retreat-from-Moscow

Britannica, T. Editors of Encyclopaedia. (n.d.). *Napoleonic wars - the treaty of Amiens. Encyclopedia Britannica*. https://www.britannica.com/event/Napoleonic-Wars/The-Treaty-of-Amiens

Britannica, T. Editors of Encyclopaedia. (2022). *Budapest. Encyclopædia Britannica*. https://www.britannica.com/place/Budapest

Britannica, T. Editors of Encyclopaedia. (2019). *Silesia historical region, Europe. Encyclopædia Britannica.* https://www.britannica.com/place/Silesia

Britannica, T. Editors of Encyclopaedia. (n.d.). *Würzburg. Encyclopedia Britannica.* https://www.britannica.com/place/Wurzburg

Brittain, R. (2010, September 21). *Smetana ~ moldau.* [Video]. YouTube. https://youtu.be/3G4NKzmfC-Q

Brownlow, M. (2022, May 20). *Franz Joseph: What you need to know.* Visiting Vienna. https://www.visitingvienna.com/culture/franz-joseph/

Budapest.com. (1995). *Budapest history – history of Budapest, Hungary.* budapest.com. https://www.budapest.com/city_guide/general_information/history.en.html

Captivating History. (2021). *The rise and fall of the Habsburg empire.* [Video]. YouTube. https://youtu.be/nMcCHDg44ek

Captivating History. (2022, April). *History of Austria: Facts, rulers & wars.* [Video]. YouTube. https://youtu.be/AOgudAhPO2Y

Castello del belvedere. (2022, September 6). In *Wikipedia.* https://it.wikipedia.org/wiki/Castello_del_Belvedere

Catherine of Habsburg. (2014, October 2). In *Wikipedia.* https://en.wikipedia.org/wiki/Catherine_of_Austria

Civitatis. (n.d.a). *History of Budapest.* https://www.introducingbudapest.com/history

Civitatis. (n.d.b). *Prater - l'antico parco d'attrazioni di Vienna.* https://www-scoprivienna-com.translate.goog/prater?_x_tr_sl=it&_x_tr_tl=en&_x_tr_hl=en&_x_tr_pto=sc

Civitatis. (n.d.c). *Ringstrasse - la strada più famosa di vienna.* https://www-scoprivienna-com.translate.goog/ringstrasse?_x_tr_sl=it&_x_tr_tl=en&_x_tr_hl=en&_x_tr_pto=sc

Classic FM. (2022). *Johann Strauss II: a life.* https://www.classicfm.com/composers/strauss-ii/guides/johann-strauss-ii-life/

Classical Net. (1995). *Classical net - basic repertoire list - j. Strauss jr.* http://www.classical.net/music/comp.lst/straussj.php

CooksInfo. (2004, July 15). *Kaiser rolls.* https://www.cooksinfo.com/kaiser-rolls

CorsetMaster. (2021a, December 1). *Opponent of tight-lacing – tight-lacing.* Wordpress. https://tight-lacing.com/opponent-of-tight-lacing/

CorsetMaster. (2021b, December 5). *An advocate of wasp waists – tight-lacing.* Wordpress. https://tight-lacing.com/an-advocate-of-wasp-waists/

CorsetMaster. (2021c, December 8). *Search results for "the truth about tight lacing" – tight-lacing.* Wordpress. https://tight-lacing.com/?s=the+truth+about+tight+lacing

CorsetMaster. (2021d, December 25). *A lady's memories of Victorian fashions – tight-lacing.* Wordpress. https://tight-lacing.com/a-ladys-memories-of-victorian-fashions/

Counterpoint. (2020, September 20). In *Wikipedia*. https://en.wikipedi-
a.org/wiki/Counterpoint

Countries and Their Cultures. (2009). *Culture of Austria - history, people, clothing,
women, beliefs, food, customs, family, social*. Everyculture.com.
https://www.everyculture.com/A-Bo/Austria.html

Davis, L. (2014, March 17). *No, corsets did not destroy the health of Victorian women*.
Gizmodo. https://gizmodo.com/no-corsets-did-not-destroy-the-health-of-
victorian-wom-1545644060

Documentary Time. (2016, June 1). *World war 1- a BBC documentary*. [Video].
YouTube. https://youtu.be/JVJiddvX878

Duchhardt, H. (2011). *The dynastic marriage*. https://d-nb.info/1031910271/34
(29/12/2022)

Educalingo. (n.d.). Edelknabe. In *educalingo dictionary*. Retrieved February 8,
2023, from, https://educalingo.com/en/dic-de/edelknabe

Encyclopedia.com. (2014). *1878-1899: Education: Overview*. Encyclopedia.com.
https://www.encyclopedia.com/history/news-wires-white-papers-and-
books/1878-1899-education-overview

Encyclopedia.com. (2019a). *Cunarder*. Encyclopedia.com. https://www.encyclo-
pedia.com/humanities/dictionaries-thesauruses-pictures-and-press-
releases/cunarder

Encyclopedia.com. (2019b). *Industry profiles: Deep sea transportation of passengers*.
Encyclopedia.com. https://www.encyclopedia.com/economics/economics-
magazines/industry-profiles-deep-sea-transportation-passengers-0

Ephemeral New York. (2009, January 23). *Legendary Lüchow's on East 14th Street*.
https://ephemeralnewyork.wordpress.com/2009/01/23/legendary-
luchows-on-east-14th-street/

Esterhazy. (n.d.). *Familie heute*. Retrieved January 7, 2023, from http://ester-
hazy.net/familie-heute/

Esterházy. (2022, November 23). In *Wikipedia*. https://en.wikipedi-
a.org/wiki/Esterh%C3%A1zy

E.U. Recipe cards. (2015). *E.U. science hub homepage*. Joint-Research-
Centre.ec.europa.eu. https://europa.eu/expo2015/sites/de-
fault/files/files/recipes/EU-at-EXPO-Milano-2015_AUSTRIA-Bread-
Recipe.pdf%3Fv=2

Fine Art America. (2023a). *Corset ad 1890 art*. Fine Art America. https://fin-
eartamerica.com/art/corset+ad+1890

Fine Art America. (2023b). *Medical effects of corset wearing art*. Fine Art America.
https://fineartamerica.com/art/medical+effects+of+corset+wearing

Fine Art America. (2023c). *Nature versus corsets art*. Fine Art America.
https://fineartamerica.com/art/nature+versus+corsets

Finishing school. (2022, November 22). In *Wikipedia*. https://en.wikipedi-
a.org/wiki/Finishing_school

Fordham University. (n.d.). *About Fordham university Fordham*. Fordham University. https://www.fordham.edu/about/

Franz Joseph I of Austria. (2019, September 14). In *Wikipedia*. https://en.wikipedia.org/wiki/Franz_Joseph_I_of_Austria

Franz Joseph I of Austria. (2019, December 19). In *Wikiquote*. https://de.wikiquote.org/wiki/Franz_Joseph_I._von_Österreich

French cuisine. (2019, March 5). In *Wikipedia*. https://en.wikipedia.org/wiki/French_cuisine

fromhungarywithlove. (2019, February 22). *Esterházy, the most powerful family in Hungary*. fromhungarywithlove. https://fromhungarywithlove.wordpress.com/2019/02/22/esterhazy-the-most-powerful-family-in-hungary/

Gamble-Eddington, T. (2021). *The black experience in early to mid-20th-century Great Britain, France, and Germany: The positioning of a community as the "other."* (Publication No. 2436)[Honors Theses, Union College]. Union Digital Works. https://digitalworks.union.edu/theses/2436?utm_source=digital works.union.edu%2Ftheses%2F2436&utm _medium=PDF&utm_campaign=PDFCoverPages

Gannet, H. (2009). *Map of the foreign-born population of the United States, 1900*. The Gilder Lehrman Institute of American History. https://www.gilderlehrman.org/history-resources/spotlight-primary-source/map-foreign-born-population-united-states-1900

German for English Speakers. (n.d.). *Diminutive endings*. German for English Speakers. http://germanforenglishspeakers.com/nouns/diminutive-endings/

Gesinde. (2022, November 7). In *Wikipedia*. https://de.wikipedia.org/wiki/Gesinde

Gjenvick-Gjønvik Archives. (2023). *Ellis island immigration experience*. G.G. Archives. https://www.ggarchives.com/Immigration/EllisIsland/index.html

Goldberg, J. (2015, May 29). *Did corsets harm women's health?* Books, Health and History. https://nyamcenterforhistory.org/2015/05/29/did-corsets-harm-womens-health/

Göttingen. (2019, October 27). In *Wikipedia*. https://en.wikipedia.org/wiki/Göttingen

Goulash. (2021, September 5). In *Wikipedia*. https://en.wikipedia.org/wiki/Goulash

Gruber, S. (2023). *Death of a European traveller*. Die Welt Der Habsburger. https://www.habsburger.net/en/chapter/death-european-traveller

Hansel and Gretel (opera). (2021, May 3). In *Wikipedia*. https://en.wikipedia.org/wiki/Hansel_and_Gretel_(opera)

History of Western Civilization. (2019). *The iron curtain history of Western civilization II*. Lumenlearning.com. https://courses.lumenlearning.com/suny-hccc-worldhistory2/chapter/the-iron-curtain/

History Tea Time with Lindsay Holiday. (2020, February 4). *Empress Elisabeth "Sisi" of Austria*. [Video]. YouTube. https://youtu.be/PiYVXDMcQyQ

History.com Editors. (2010, March 3). *Emperor of Mexico executed*. History. https://www.history.com/this-day-in-history/emperor-of-mexico-executedHistory.com Editors. (2009, October 29). *U.S. immigration before 1965*. History. https://www.history.com/topics/immigration/u-s-immigration-before-1965#section_4

History.com Editors. (2010, February 9). *Napoleon's Grande Armee invades Russia*. History. https://www.history.com/this-day-in-history/napoleons-grande-armee-invades-russia

History.com Editors. (2018, August 21). *Ellis island*. History. https://www.history.com/topics/immigration/ellis-island

Hofburg. (2021, May 29). In *Wikipedia*. https://en.wikipedia.org/wiki/Hofburg

Hofzuckerbäcker, K. (2022). *Demel through the centuries*. Demel Wien. https://www.demel.com/pages/demels-history

Höhere Mädchenschule. (2019, April 17). In *Wikipedia*. https://en.wikipedia.org/wiki/H%C3%B6here_M%C3%A4dchenschule

House of Habsburg. (2019, December 8). In *Wikipedia*. https://en.wikipedia.org/wiki/House_of_Habsburg

Humanities West. (2016, November 5). *Vienna on the verge (1890-1918) | November 4-5, 2016*. Humanities West. https://humanitieswest.org/vienna-on-the-verge-1890-1918/

Huntsberger, A. (2021, March 18). *Love and money: a brief history of dowries*. OppLoans. https://www.opploans.com/oppu/articles/love-and-money-a-brief-history-of-dowries/

Kouli, Y. (2017). The German minority in Poland between 1945 and 1960: A key element of Poland's postwar economy. *Region: Regional Studies of Russia, Eastern Europe, and Central Asia*, *6*(1), 29–53. https://doi.org/10.1353/reg.2017.0002

Kulik, R. M. (2022, November 30). *Lady-in-waiting*. Britannica. https://www.britannica.com/topic/lady-in-waiting

Kurlander, E. (2002). Nationalism, ethnic preoccupation, and the decline of German liberalism: A Silesian case study, 1898–1933. *Historian*, *65*(1), 95–121. https://doi.org/10.1111/1540-6563.651018

Lansdale, M. H. (1902). *The Vienna opera house, c. 1900*. TOTA. https://www.tota.world/article/3544/

Legends of America. (2023). *Soldiers and officers in American history*. Legends of America. https://www.legendsofamerica.com/soldier-list/

Liegnitz (region). (2021, August 3). In *Wikipedia*. https://en.m.wikipedia.org/wiki/Liegnitz_(region)

Linguee Dictionary. (2023). *Herrschaftshaus - English translation*. Linguee. https://www.linguee.com/german-english/translation/herrschaftshaus.html

List of diminutives by language. (2022, November 13). In *Wikipedia*. https://en.wikipedia.org/wiki/List_of_diminutives_by_language#Yiddish

Little Germany, Manhattan. (2021, June 27). In *Wikipedia*. https://en.wikipedia.org/wiki/Little_Germany

Little, B. (2019, April 2). *When German immigrants were America's undesirables*. History. https://www.history.com/news/anti-german-sentiment-wwi

Lüchow's. (2019, January 10). In *Wikipedia*. https://en.wikipedia.org/wiki/Luchow's

Lynn, E. (2010, November 16). *A short history of corsetry, from whalebone to lycra*. Slate Magazine. https://slate.com/culture/2010/11/a-short-history-of-corsetry-from-whalebone-to-lycra.html

Mapcarta. (n.d.). Mrokocin. https://mapcarta.com/N417809620

Maturi, W. (1937). *Treccani - la cultura italiana treccani, il portale del sapere*. Treccani. https://www-treccani-it.translate.goog/enciclopedia/troppau_%28Enciclopedia-Italiana%29/?_x_tr_sl=it&_x_tr_tl=en&_x_tr_hl=en&_x_tr_pto=sc

Mayerling incident. (2022, December 16). In *Wikipedia*. https://en.wikipedia.org/wiki/Mayerling_incident

Meares, H. (2018, August 22). *The tragic Austrian empress who was murdered by anarchists*. History. https://www.history.com/news/the-tragic-austrian-empress-who-was-murdered-by-anarchists

Merriam-Webster. (n.d.). Brioche. In *Merriam-Webster.com dictionary*. Retrieved January 5, 2023, from https://www.merriam-webster.com/dictionary/brioche

Merriam-Webster. (n.d.). CanCan. In *Merriam-Webster.com dictionary*. Retrieved January 5, 2023, from https://www.merriam-webster.com/dictionary/cancan

Merriam-Webster. (n.d.). Coiffure. In *Merriam-Webster.com dictionary*. https://www.merriam-webster.com/dictionary/coiffure

Merriam-Webster. (n.d.). Croissant. In *Merriam-Webster.com dictionary*. Retrieved January 5, 2023, from https://www.merriam-webster.com/dictionary/croissant

Merriam-Webster. (n.d.). Éclat. In *Merriam-Webster.com dictionary*. Retrieved January 5, 2023, from https://www.merriam-webster.com/dictionary/%C3%A9clat

Merriam-Webster. (n.d.). En route. In *Merriam-Webster.com dictionary*. Retrieved January 5, 2023, from https://www.merriam-webster.com/dictionary/en%20route

Merriam-Webster. (n.d.). Entree. In *Merriam-Webster.com dictionary*. Retrieved January 5, 2023, from https://www.merriam-webster.com/dictionary/entr%C3%A9e

Merriam-Webster. (n.d.). Fashionista. In *Merriam-Webster.com dictionary*.

Retrieved January 5, 2023, from https://www.merriam-webster.com/dictionary/fashionista

Merriam-Webster. (n.d.). Faux pas. In *Merriam-Webster.com dictionary*. Retrieved January 5, 2023, from https://www.merriam-webster.com/dictionary/faux%20pas

Merriam-Webster. (n.d.). Grande dame. In *Merriam-Webster.com dictionary*. Retrieved January 5, 2023, from https://www.merriam-webster.com/dictionary/grande%20dame

Merriam-Webster. (n.d.). Haute couture. In *Merriam-Webster.com dictionary*. Retrieved January 5, 2023, from https://www.merriam-webster.com/dictionary/haute%20couture

Merriam-Webster. (n.d.). Kipfel. In *Merriam-Webster.com dictionary*. Retrieved January 5, 2023, from https://www.merriam-webster.com/dictionary/kipfel

Merriam-Webster. (n.d.). Knödel. In *Merriam-Webster.com dictionary*. Retrieved January 5, 2023, from https://www.merriam-webster.com/dictionary/kn%C3%B6del

Merriam-Webster. (n.d.). Loge. In *Merriam-Webster.com dictionary*. Retrieved January 5, 2023, from https://www.merriam-webster.com/dictionary/loge

Merriam-Webster. (n.d.). Modiste. In *Merriam-Webster.com dictionary*. https://www.merriam-webster.com/dictionary/modiste

Merriam-Webster. (n.d.). Opéra comique. In *Merriam-Webster.com dictionary*. Retrieved January 5, 2023, from https://www.merriam-webster.com/dictionary/op%C3%A9ra%20comique

Merriam-Webster. (n.d.). Objet d'art. In *Merriam-Webster.com dictionary*. Retrieved January 5, 2023, from https://www.merriam-webster.com/dictionary/objet%20d%27art

Merriam-Webster. (n.d.). Par excellence. In *Merriam-Webster.com dictionary*. Retrieved January 5, 2023, from https://www.merriam-webster.com/dictionary/par%20excellence

Merriam-Webster. (n.d.). Per capita. In *Merriam-Webster.com dictionary*. Retrieved January 5, 2023, from https://www.merriam-webster.com/dictionary/per%20capita

Merriam-Webster. (n.d.). Umlaut. In *Merriam-Webster.com dictionary*. Retrieved January 5, 2023, from https://www.merriam-webster.com/dictionary/umlaut

Metropolitan Museum of Art, & Blum, S. (1979). *Fashions of the Habsburg era: Austria-Hungary*. Google Books. https://books.google.it/books?printsec=frontcover&id=ovQm_TWOIzgC&redir_esc=y#v=onepage&q&f=fals

Mrokocin. (2020a, October 6). In *Wikipedia*. https://en.wikipedia.org/wiki/Mrokocin

Mullin, E. (2016, May 10). *How Tuberculosis Shaped Victorian Fashion*. Smithsonian.   https://www.smithsonianmag.com/science-nature/how-tuberculosis-shaped-victorian-fashion-180959029/

Mutschlechner, M. (2022a). *The allure of the exotic – Habsburgs and the fashion for all things Chinese*. Die Welt Der Habsburger. https://www.habsburger.net/en/chapter/allure-exotic-habsburgs-and-fashion-all-things-chinese

Mutschlechner, M. (2022b). *The "first tier" of society - social interaction in the aristocracy*. Die Welt Der Habsburger. https://www.habsburger.net/en/chapter/first-tier-society-social-interaction-aristocracy

Mutschlechner, M. (2023a). *A year at court – the court calendar*. Die Welt Der Habsburger.   https://www.habsburger.net/en/chapter/year-court-court-calendar

Mutschlechner, M. (2023b). *Archduke Franz Ferdinand – heir to the throne*. Die Welt Der Habsburger. https://www.habsburger.net/en/chapter/archduke-franz-ferdinand-heir-throne

Mutschlechner, M. (2023c). Elisabeth and Franz Joseph: Wedding and marriage. *Die Welt Der Habsburger*. https://www.habsburger.net/en/chapter/elisabeth-and-franz-joseph-wedding-and-marriage

Mutschlechner, M. (2023d). *Elisabeth's childhood*. Die Welt Der Habsburger. https://www.habsburger.net/en/chapter/elisabeths-childhood

Mutschlechner, M. (2023e). *Elisabeth's eccentric lifestyle*. Die Welt Der Habsburger. https://www.habsburger.net/en/chapter/elisabeths-eccentric-lifestyle

Mutschlechner, M. (2023f). *Elisabeth's transformation*. Die Welt Der Habsburger. https://www.habsburger.net/en/chapter/elisabeths-transformation

Mutschlechner, M. (2023g). *Franz Ferdinand: The conservative archduke*. Die Welt Der Habsburger. https://www.habsburger.net/en/chapter/franz-ferdinand-conservative-archduke

Mutschlechner, M. (2023h). *Franz Joseph and Franz Ferdinand – a tense relationship*. Die Welt Der Habsburger. https://www.habsburger.net/en/chapter/franz-joseph-and-franz-ferdinand-tense-relationship

Mutschlechner, M. (2023i). *Franz Joseph: The very model of an emperor*. Die Welt Der Habsburger. https://www.habsburger.net/en/chapter/franz-joseph-very-model-emperor

Mutschlechner, M. (2023j). *Members only – the right of admission to Court*. Die Welt Der Habsburger. https://www.habsburger.net/en/chapter/members-only-right-admission-court

Mutschlechner, M. (2023k). *The court kitchens – dining at the emperor's behest*. Die Welt Der Habsburger. https://www.habsburger.net/en/chapter/court-kitchens-dining-emperors-behest

Mutschlechner, M. (2023l). *The subtle distinction: Court ball and ball at Court*. Die Welt Der Habsburger. https://www.habsburger.net/en/chapter/subtle-distinction-court-ball-and-ball-court

My German Recipes. (2019, October 20). *How to make German kaiser rolls, hand-crafted*   ✪   *MyGerman.recipes.*   [Video].   YouTube.
https://youtu.be/FiqV2B8bF-g

National Geographic Society. (2022, May 20). *Growth of Colonial Settlement.*
https://education.nationalgeographic.org/resource/colonial-settlement

National Geographic Society. (n.d.). *Population distribution 17th-19th century.*
https://education.nationalgeographic.org/resource/resource-library-popu-lation-distribution-17th-19th

National Geographic Society. (2014, November 14). *A Taste of Old World Europe:
Wiener   Schnitzel.*   https://www.nationalgeographic.com/travel/article/a-taste-of-old-world-europe-wiener-schnitzel

National Geographic Society. (2022, May 20). *Immigration to the U.S. in the late
1800s.*
https://education.nationalgeographic.org/resource/immigration-1870-1900

Northwoods Star Journal. (2012, June 13). *Historically speaking: Language chal-lenges   for   early   immigrants.*   Star   Journal.   https://starjournalnow.-com/2012/06/13/historically-speaking-language-challenges-for-early-immigrants/

Offenbach, Jacques. (2022, December 31). In *Wikipedia.* https://en.wikipedi-a.org/wiki/Jacques_Offenbach

Ohajuru, M. (2013, August 9). *[King Magi] The Black Magus (ca. 1350-).* BlackPast.
https://www.blackpast.org/global-african-history/black-magus-c-1350/

Palmer, A. (2021, June 2). *A 19th-century whalebone corset.* Royal Ontario
Museum.   https://www.rom.on.ca/en/collections-research/magazine/a-19th-century-whalebone-corset

Passionsspiele Oberammergau. (2022). *Home.* Passion Play 2022. https://www.-passionsspiele-oberammergau.de/en/home

Peoplepill. (n.d.). *Margaret Matzenauer: American opera singer (1881 - 1963).*
Peoplepill. https://peoplepill.com/people/margaret-matzenauer

Prater. (2019, October 14). In *Wikipedia.* https://en.wikipedia.org/wiki/Prater

Prentice Hall. (2018, November 17). In *Wikipedia.* https://en.wikipedi-a.org/wiki/Prentice_Hall

Presto Music. (2002). *Joseph Franz Karl Lanner (composer).* Presto Music.
https://www.prestomusic.com/classical/composers/1157--lanner

Pryce-Jones, D. (2022). *National review.* (19th ed., Vol. 74). National Review,
Inc., Etc.

Real Royalty. (2022, March). *Why Empress Sissi escaped to Venice On Sissi's Traces
Real Royalty* [Video]. YouTube. https://youtu.be/qAhRyFcyvfo

Rogers, S. (2021, March 5). *Winston Churchill's iron curtain speech—March 5, 1946.*
The National WWII Museum New Orleans. https://www.nationalww2mu-seum.org/war/articles/winston-churchills-iron-curtain-speech-march-5-1946

Rosen, B. (2016, November 21). Zum 100. Todestag von Franz Joseph I. Kaiser-Dämmerung. *Der Tagesspiegel Online*. https://www.-tagesspiegel.de/gesellschaft/kaiser-dammerung-3775522.html

Rossignol, S. (2022). *Silesia: A Brief Overview*. Mapping Eastern Europe. https://mappingeasterneurope.princeton.edu/item/silesia-a-brief-overview.html

Rudolf, crown prince of Austria. (2022, December 1). In *Wikipedia*. https://en.wikipedia.org/wiki/Rudolf

Schulz, D. (2014, October 2). *Kleindeutschland: The history of the east village's little Germany*. 6sqft. https://www.6sqft.com/kleindeutschland-the-history-of-the-east-villages-little-germany/

Schulz, D. (2015, February 3). *Then and Now: From Luchow's German Restaurant to NYU Dorm*. 6sqft. https://www.6sqft.com/then-now-from-luchows-german-restaurant-to-nyu-dorm/

Schulze, M.-S. . (2000). Patterns of growth and stagnation in the late nineteenth century Habsburg economy. *European Review of Economic History, 4*(3), 311–340. https://doi.org/10.1017/s1361491600000095

See U in History/Mythology. (2021a). *House of Habsburg: The greatest dynasty of Europe - see u in history*. [Video]. YouTube. https://youtu.be/0fjtp1HkhZk

See U in History/Mythology. (2021b). *The Habsburg dynasty - the decline of the greatest monarchical house in Europe - see u in history*. [Video]. YouTube. https://youtu.be/e0s33B-jEqQ

Şengün, E. (2022, November 24). Anthropology: The centuries-old tradition of molybdomancy or lead-pouring. *Yoair Blog*. https://www.yoair.-com/blog/anthropology-the-centuries-old-tradition-of-molybdomancy-or-lead-pouring/

Silesia. (2023, February 3). In *Wikipedia*. https://en.wikipedia.org/wiki/Silesia

Smith, M. (2021, February 12). A hatful of horror: The Victorian headwear craze that led to mass slaughter. HistoryExtra. https://www.historyextra.-com/period/victorian/victorian-hats-birds-feathered-hat-fashion/

Smithsonian American Art Museum. (n.d.). *Immigration in the early 20th century*. SAAM. https://americanexperience.si.edu/wp-content/uploads/2013/11/Immigration-in-the-Early-20th-Century_.pdf

Stadtprozelten. (2021, December 4). In *Wikipedia*. https://en.wikipedia.org/wiki/Stadtprozelten

Starnegg, B. (2020, April 2). *Sissi facts, part II 5 more things you didn't know about empress Elisabeth of Austria*. Vienna in English. https://metropole.at/sissi-facts-part-2-empress-elisabeth-of-austria/

TasteAtlas. (2023). *Krapfen*. tasteatlas. https://www.tasteatlas.com/krapfen

The Bartered Bride. (2020, October 15). In *Wikipedia*. https://en.wikipedia.org/wiki/The_Bartered_Bride

The Economist. (2016, December 24). *How Vienna produced ideas that shaped the west*. The Economist. https://www.economist.com/christmas-specials/2016/12/24/how-vienna-produced-ideas-that-shaped-the-west

The Great War. (2022, July 15). *Why did the first world war break out? (July crisis 1914 documentary)*. [Video]. YouTube. https://youtu.be/9KESpCFmYMk

The Metropolitan Opera. (2023). *Hansel and Gretel*. https://www.metopera.org/user-information/old-seasons/2020-21/hansel-and-gretel/

The Musician. (2019, April). *Il musicalista Joseph Lanner*. https://www-ilpostalista-it.translate.goog/musicalista/musica1904.htm?_x_tr_sl=it&_x_tr_tl=en&_x_tr_hl=en&_x_tr_pto=sc

The National Archives. (1946, March 5). *The national archives - homepage*. The National Archives. https://www.nationalarchives.gov.uk/education/resources/cold-war-on-file/iron-curtain-speech/

The New York Times. (1979, October 25). B.F. Herberick, retired from conference board. *The New York Times*. https://www.nytimes.com/1979/10/25/archives/bf-herberick-retired-from-conference-board.html

The Statue of Liberty–Ellis Island Foundation. (2020, March 16). *Family History Center*. https://www.statueofliberty.org/ellis-island/family-history-center/

The World of Habsburgs. (2022). *Franz Joseph I*. Die Welt Der Habsburger. https://www.habsburger.net/en/persons/habsburg-emperor/franz-joseph-i

The World of Habsburgs. (2023a). *An all too closed society*. Die Welt Der Habsburger. https://www.habsburger.net/en/chapter/all-too-closed-society

The World of Habsburgs. (2023b). *Elisabeth*. Die Welt Der Habsburger. https://www.habsburger.net/en/persons/habsburg/elisabeth

The World of Habsburgs. (2023c). *Empress Elizabeth*. Die Welt Der Habsburger. https://www.habsburger.net/en/search?s=+empress+elisabeth

The World of the Habsburgs. (2022a). *The Vienna Hofburg*. Die Welt Der Habsburger. https://www.habsburger.net/en/locations/vienna-hofburg

The World of the Habsburgs. (2022b). *Vienna – Schönbrunn Palace*. Die Welt Der Habsburger. https://www.habsburger.net/en/locations/vienna-schoenbrunn-palace

The World of the Habsburgs. (2023a). *Franz Ferdinand*. Die Welt Der Habsburger. https://www.habsburger.net/en/persons/habsburg/franz-ferdinand

The World of the Habsburgs. (2023b). *High society – social life in the imperial capital*. Die Welt Der Habsburger. https://www.habsburger.net/en/stories/high-society-social-life-imperial-capital

Trümmerfrau. (2020, February 24). In *Wikipedia*. https://en.wikipedia.org/wiki/Trümmerfrau

UNESCO Courier. (2021, June 17). *Olivette Otele: "The history of Europe's blacks has been struck by a partial amnesia."* UNESCO. https://en.unesco.org/courier/2021-3/olivette-otele-history-europes-blacks-has-been-struck-partial-amnesia

Vienna. (2018, September 10). *Sisi - empress Elisabeth of Austria* [Video]. YouTube. https://youtu.be/R2Uplm7fbQo

Vienna Now Forever. (n.d.a). *Belvedere – Palace and Museum.* https://www.wien.info/en/sightseeing/museums-exhibitions/top/belvedere-341062

Vienna Now Forever. (n.d.b). *The origin of the Ringstrasse.* https://www.wien.info/en/sightseeing/ringstrasse/construction-of-ringstrasse-343606

Vienna Ring Road. (2022, December 22). In *Wikipedia.* https://en.wikipedia.org/wiki/Vienna_Ring_Road

Vienna Volksoper. (2021, April 21). In *Wikipedia.* https://en.wikipedia.org/wiki/Vienna_Volksoper

Volynsky, M. (2012, November 24). *The emperor's schnitzel: Food in the Austro-Hungarian empire.* Radio Prague International. https://english.radio.cz/emperors-schnitzel-food-austro-hungarian-empire-8549340

Westminster College. (2019). *Churchill's iron curtain speech.* https://www.wcmo.edu/about/history/iron-curtain-speech.html

Wiesner, Ruff, & Wheeler. (2004). *Discovering the Western Past: A Look at the Evidence Vienna and Paris, 1850-1930: The development of the modern city.* (Volume II, 5th edition). Boston: Houghton Mifflin. http://mprapeuro.weebly.com/uploads/2/9/3/0/29308547/vienna_paris_documents.pdf

Würzburg. (2019, March 8). In *Wikipedia.* https://en.wikipedia.org/wiki/Wurzburg

IMAGE REFERENCES

Allstar Picture Library Ltd. (2023). *Bedrich Smetana composer (1874)* [Image]. Alamy. https://c8.alamy.com/compes/bptm-f1/bedrich-smetana-compositor-1874-bptmf1.jpg

Chronicle. (n.d.). Archduke Franz Ferdinand [Image]. Alamy. https://www.alamy.com/archduke-franz-ferdinand-image6068030.html

Chronicle. (2015). *Luchow's Famous Restaurant, New York City, USA* [Image]. Alamy. https://www.alamy.com/stock-photo-luchows-famous-restaurant-new-york-city-usa-105389817.html

history_docu_photo. (2020). *Johann Strauss II or Johann Strauss Jr., 1825 – 1899, Austrian composer of light music* [Image]. Alamy. https://www.alamy.com/johann-strauss-ii-or-johann-strauss-jr-1825-1899-austrian-composer-of-light-music-image359554643.html

INTERFOTO. (n.d.). *Matzenauer, Margarethe, 1.6.1881 - 19.5.1963, German singer (contralto/mezzo-soprano), half length, als "Waltraute" in opera cycle "The Ring of the Nibelung" by Richard Wagner* [Image]. Alamy. https://www.alamy.com/stock-photo-matzenauer-margarethe-161881-1951963-german-singer-contraltomezzo-47983806.html

Library of Congress. (n.d.). *Elizabeth -- Murdered Empress of Austria* [Image]. Alamy. https://www.alamy.com/stock-photo-elizabeth-murdered-empress-of-austria-loc-55117055.html

Maras. (1930-1935). *Schloss Bruckstein* [Image]. Polska.org.pl. https://polska-org.pl/5997607,foto.html

Mayer, B. (2021). *Vienna State Opera House* [Image]. Unsplash. https://unsplash.com/s/photos/vienna-state-opera-house

McCourt Collection, Courtesy of the. (2022) *Fabian Bachrach portrait of Bernard Herberick; Albertina Zimmerman, beloved Oma; Grandfather Anton Zimmerman; August, Crescentia, and Hans; Hans; Albertina and Hans; Marlboro Public School; Crescentia, Oma, and Hans, in 1939 at Crescentia's home in Marlborough, New York. Sons Hans and August visited the U.S. prior to World War II* [Images].

Sueddeutsche Zeitung Photo. (n.d.). *Emperor Franz Joseph I (1830-1916) and Empress Elisabeth of Austria (1837-1898)* [Image]. Alamy. https://www.alamy.com/emperor-franz-joseph-i-1830-1916-and-empress-elisabeth-of-austria-1837-1898-image247137833.html

The New York Public Library. (2020). *Ellis island - ready for travel and going north, south and west. Immigrants with baggage lined up at teller's windows marked money exchange. 1910* [Image]. Unsplash. https://unsplash.com/photos/MiVrRlSe4BI

The Pioneer of the Marlborough High School, Vol 5, no. 1. (1927). *David D. Taylor, the Principal at Marlborough High School.* [Image].

Universal Images Group North America LLC. (n.d.). *Corset le Furet* [Image]. Alamy. https://www.alamy.com/corset-le-furet-image402610985.html

ABOUT THE AUTHORS

Bernard F. Herberick (1910–1979), known as Barney, was Oma's grandson. He shared recollections of Oma's memories with the family. He also aimed to publish his manuscript about her life in Reader's Digest, but, sadly, it was rejected. It remained with the family until now.

On October 25, 1979, his obituary was published on page 26 of the New York Times as follows (The New York Times, 1979):

> Bernard F. Herberick, former executive director of operations and services of the Conference Board, a non-profit business and economic research organization in New York, died Monday at Stamford (Conn.) Hospital. He was 69 years old and lived in Darien, Conn.
>
> Mr. Herberick joined the Conference Board in 1946, when it was known as the National Industrial Conference Board. In the beginning he was director of its news department. He held various other positions, including assistant vice president of production, before taking over the operations services department. When he retired in 1971 he joined the Council of Better Business Bureaus as director of special projects.
>
> Mr. Herberick was born in Marlborough, N.Y. He received a bachelor's degree in economics from Fordham University, and a master's degree in foreign service at Georgetown University.
>
> During World War II he served with the Office of Strategic Services, and was forward intelligence officer in the [China-Burma-India] Theater.

Mr. Herberick is survived by his wife, the former Lucy Rosser; a son, James of New Milford, Conn.; a sister Virginia McCourt of Marlborough, and two grandchildren.

D. Herberick, contributing author, is one of Bernard's grandchildren.

NOTES

1. GROWING UP

1. In Oma's day, the word *gypsies* was used. Today the acceptable term is *Roma*.
2. *Bleigiessen* with lead has been banned in the European Union since 2018 owing to the poisonous lead vapor. Alternatives are available, see Bölükbasi.
3. Albert of Saxe-Coburg had a German background and was introduced to the Queen by his Belgian uncle, Leopold. As consort, he advised and assisted Queen Victoria with domestic reforms. His liberal views supported emancipation, the welfare of the working class, better schooling, and technological advancement. His early death at 42 profoundly shocked Queen Victoria, who wore black for the rest of her life. His public image improved significantly after his passing. His legacy left a string of monarchs and royal and noble descendants throughout Europe.

3. TO THE MANOR BORN

1. Göttingen is a city in Lower Saxony, part of central Germany, situated on the Leine river. It's about 100 km south of Hannover. The city gained prosperity when the University of Göttingen was established in 1737, which became one of the most famous universities in Europe and remains one of the top-ranking global universities today. The university prides itself on one of the richest library collections in Germany. Apart from the university's prestige, the city was fairly undamaged by the world wars, and its medieval architecture and gothic churches remained intact. Furthermore, it offers diverse industries apart from being a "scholarly" city, mainly in advanced technologies of optical precision instruments (e.g., Carl Zeiss, Inc.), chemicals, synthetics, and publishing. The city still bears a solid scholarly element.
2. Würzburg is a glamorous Baroque city in the northwestern part of Bavaria in south-central Germany. It is approximately 120 km southeast of Frankfurt am Main, spanning the river Main—a tributary of the Rhine river. It started as a Celtic settlement in the early 700s and, after years of political turmoil, eventually passed to Bavaria in the early 1800s. It is mainly an administrative capital and boasting wine and printing industries. The present university of Würzburg was reinstated in 1582 after a previous one only existed for a few years. Today, Würzburg hosts a multitude of medieval architectural landmarks, including the Main Bridge.

4. EVER-RELIABLE, UNFAILING CURE

1. The Ringstrasse is Vienna's most famous street and was an urban planning masterpiece inspired in 1857 by Emperor Franz Joseph to connect the rest of the city with the imperial quarters, which were, until then, firmly hidden behind the city walls. It took 50 years to complete the circular boulevard, which until this day, remains one of the most impressive in the world. With this, he opened the aristocratic society to the Haute bourgeoisie and the Jewish bourgeoisie. He added to the grandeur of the Habsburg empire
2. The Prater is the large amusement park in Vienna, Austria, that includes the famous Wiener Riesenrad Ferris wheel.
3. The elaborate Viennese Schönnbrunn Palace and its exquisite gardens have become one of Austria's most frequently visited museums. It became known as a "projection surface for the Habsburg aspirations to Great Power status" (The World of the Habsburgs, 2022) with its grandiose designs.
4. Hofburg is a sprawling architectural masterpiece that dominates the historic city center of Vienna. It has developed over the 700-year reign of the Habsburgs into the most famous palace of their remarkable dynasty after its birth in the 13th century. Schönnbrunn was the summer residence of the Habsburgs, while Hofburg was visited during the freezing winter months. The imperial palace still serves as an official residence of the president of Austria. Also, it houses various art museums, an imperial library, the Burgtheater, and the famous Spanish Riding School.
5. The lavish splendor of the Belvedere Palace is a Baroque masterpiece that houses impressive art museums today.

6. SUCH PEOPLE

1. The Liegnitz area stretched along the Kaczawa river and bordered Poland to the northeast, the Province of Brandenburg to the northwest, Saxony to the west, and Bohemia (later known as Czechoslovakia) to the south. It became a vital trading center, and the textile industry remains strong to this day. The town became another Habsburg entity in 1675. It was an administrative region of the Province of Lower Silesia but sadly suffered extensive damage during World War II. Nowadays, it's known as Legnica in southwestern Poland.
2. The final blow was the death of the Archduke in Sarajevo, discussed later. After that, the Habsburg monarchy died a quick death: Austria declared war against Serbia, World War I erupted, Franz Joseph died in 1916, and the first Austrian republic was established at the end of the war in 1918, which dissolved the influential reign of the Habsburg dynasty. Massive inflation, unemployment, and an economy on the brink of collapse gave rise to an uncertain future. The early 1930s brought economic depression and a

declaration of martial law to protect the country against Hitler, which lasted until 1938 when Austria was incorporated into the German Reich. After World War II, Austria was managed by the victorious Allies (the US, UK, Soviet Union, and France) for ten years. Austria soon declared its neutrality and, due to its geo-political position close to the Iron Curtain, granted asylum to refugees from Communist countries.

3. *Snackl coined* by Oma—snack in the diminutive form.

EPILOGUE

1. Other ethnic groups were mostly Slovenian, Croatian, Hungarian, Slovakian, and Czech minorities. Gypsies and people of Jewish descent who lived in Austria for many years were considered minority groups.

Made in the USA
Las Vegas, NV
30 March 2025

20296145R00069